To my friend in
" GOD IS ?
1. COR. 1. 9
Ron Jones 23/11/08

THEN SOMETHING REMARKABLE HAPPENED!
RON JONES
His autobiography
(with Paul Davis)

Printed by Antony Rowe Ltd, Eastbourne

Published by Crossbridge Books
345 Old Birmingham Road
Bromsgrove, B60 1NX
Tel: 0121 447 7897

ISBN 0 9549708 0 2

British Library Cataloguing in Publication Data.
A catalogue record for this book is available from the British Library.

Also published by Crossbridge Books:

Stepping-Stone Miracles Des Morton
The God of Miracles Trevor and Anne Dearing
Schizophrenia Defeated James Stacey
Mountains on the Moon Michael Arthern
First Century Close-ups Roger Penney
Called to Be a Wife Anne Dearing
Always Here For You Trevor Dearing

The Autobiography of Ron Jones

THEN SOMETHING REMARKABLE HAPPENED!
RON JONES
(with Paul Davis)

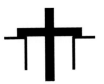

CROSSBRIDGE BOOKS

PREFACE

A good leader, if offered the choice between power and influence, will always choose the latter. There are those who enjoy a level of authority that emanates out of the 'office that they hold' but who have little personal influence over those around them. Others hold no position at all but nevertheless affect the lives of many through challenge, inspiration and encouragement.

Ron Jones, throughout a long, rich and varied ministry, has exercised both qualities. He has risen to the highest position within his denomination but, outside the sphere of hierarchical authority, has touched the lives of multitudes. Some of these have been members of churches he has pastored, but the majority are leaders across the denominations and throughout the world.

When I entered the pastoral ministry in the early seventies he was leading one of Elim's flagship churches – the City Temple in Bristol. There were perhaps six people who shaped my understanding of 'church' and 'ministry' in those days and Ron Jones was numbered high among them. Many of my contemporaries would have been similarly influenced.

Ron was, and remains to this day in 2005, one of the finest communicators I have ever known. Whether the arena was the pulpit or the mass media, the scenario was the same – the capacity to link with his audience as if he was sitting with them in their own home. The gift of incisive leadership to the 'crowd' married to a warm relational connection with the individual is talent reserved for only a few.

At the commencement of my ministry I considered him a mentor. Today, he remains my very dear friend. Most of all, he is a man committed to a commission that God gave him in his earliest years. He is a flame that refuses to dim – even in advancing years.

Reverend John Glass
(General Superintendent of the Elim Pentecostal Churches, UK)

Acknowledgements

Paul Davis
Mervyn Douglas
John Glass
Stephen Hilliard
David Holmes
Wynne Lewis
Desmond Morton
Gerald Williams
David Woodfield

Bible Quotations
King James Version
New King James Version

MY SINCEREST THANKS TO ALL WHO HELPED ME TO
MAKE THIS BOOK POSSIBLE;
MY FERVENT PRAYER: THAT GOD WILL USE THIS
BOOK TO ENCOURAGE, INSPIRE AND CHALLENGE ALL
WHO READ IT.

Ron Jones.

FOREWORD
by
SELWYN HUGHES

Someone has said that a Christian autobiography is like a child being offered to the world not knowing how it will serve the good of God.

There is no doubt in my mind however, that Ron Jones' autobiography will serve God's goodness in a most definite and positive way and will draw many to the high calling of living-out their lives at full stretch in the service of the Master. There is not a man amongst the evangelists of the 20th century who has done more to win people to Christ and then nurture them in the faith than Ron! His indefatigable zeal-for-Christ and the energy which he has displayed in serving the Saviour will live long in the minds of those who have known him.

I became a firsthand observer of Ron's pastoral abilities when I took over the spiritual responsibilities of a church at which he, a few years previously, had been the pastor. It was obvious from the first few days that I settled in the church how Ron's spiritual influence and dynamism continued to have an effect on the congregation. I was able to build on the foundation that he had laid and I shall ever be grateful to him for making my life as a young pastor easier than it might have been.

Later when I met Ron and came to know more about him, his character and abilities marked him out as a spiritual leader in God's timepiece of redemption. His story of God's leading and interventions in his life despite a number of setbacks will, I know, inspire many a soul (especially young ministers) whose footsteps may be flagging along the way.

The teasing title, *"Then something remarkable happened!"* beckons us to look through the window of God's sovereignty and see some of the surprises that He has in store for those who follow Him and trust Him.

I commend this book to all Christians everywhere. May it serve the goodness of God in ways beyond all telling.

(Selwyn Hughes' ministry with CWR and through the daily readings entitled 'Every Day with Jesus' has brought many blessings to millions of people throughout the world.)

INTRODUCTION 1
by
WYNNE LEWIS

This is a riveting account of a man mightily used of God to bring many hundreds to faith in Christ, a man who would prove to be one of the most significant Pentecostal leaders in the twentieth century. From very humble beginnings and against tremendous odds, God enabled him to reach the heights of service for his Lord and Saviour. This is an inspiring story that will encourage many others to live a life of commitment, dedication and enthusiasm for God.

Ron Jones has pastored some of the largest churches in the United Kingdom and his enthusiasm as an evangelist resulted in the planting of several new churches. His warm, friendly disposition has gained him thousands of friends throughout the world. His vivid imaginative preaching has impacted large gatherings in London's Royal Albert Hall and the World Pentecostal Conference. In recognition of his outstanding leadership skills, the Conference of the Elim Pentecostal Churches UK elected him as its president on two occasions, and in 1978 it appointed him as the General Superintendent of the denomination.

This book could encourage you to similarly dedicate your life to the service of the King of Kings.

(Wynne Lewis is a well-known international speaker and served as the General Superintendent of the Elim Pentecostal churches.)

INTRODUCTION 2
by
GERALD WILLIAMS

God makes His disciples in all shapes and sizes and no two are the same. He makes the 'bookish academic', and the 'rough-and-ready'. He chooses from the rich and from the poor. Then there are the 'indestructible stayers' who are the marathon men and women of His Kingdom. Ron Jones is one of them.

When I first met him for one of his Sky TV interviews, I felt in awe of the long haul he's on for Christ. He has been in ministry for over 64 years and is still in wonderment at what God does.

Ron is an overcomer and an inspiration. He has a wealth of tales to tell and all of them to the Father's glory.

(For many years, Gerald Williams was the tennis correspondent for BBC Television and Radio who became well known for his Wimbledon commentary.)

INTRODUCTION 3
by
PAUL DAVIS

Among the well-known twentieth century Pentecostal Church leaders in the UK, no one was more beloved in reputation than Pastor Ron Jones. His universally popular, anecdotal preaching style was enjoyed by enthusiastic congregations all over the world.

Ron is big in personality and high in integrity. As a trail-blazer, he set for himself and his churches ever-rising standards. My friend is not just a great preacher and visionary, he is intelligent, and gracious – fully dedicated to his late wife, family and Lord.

Ron communicates powerfully in the area of story-telling, taking great delight in recounting simple, life-changing truths, as this book illustrates ... Some say that he makes the Bible characters come alive.

He has represented the Elim Church denomination interests in many parts of the globe with great dignity. Through all the changing scenes of life, Ron has striven via his gifts to bring lost souls to the Lord Jesus, bridging the gap between heaven and earth. Great is the harvest of his labours already, with much more promise to come. Without hesitation, many of his associates and congregations happily testified to this writer that Ron spiritually inspired people in many walks of life.

On a personal note, this writer must document his thanks to Ron. I found him to be a man who walked his talk, giving of his time and energy in research for this book.

(Paul Davis authored the official biographies of George Hamilton IV, Pat Boone and the Blackwood Brothers. He is pastor at Leighton Christian Fellowship, Bedfordshire, England.)

Contents

CHAPTER 1

Beginnings

Swansea in Wales was first settled by Vikings and the name is from Sweyn's oy-a which in 'Scandinavian talk' means Sweyn's Island or inlet. A Viking brooch was found on the beach at Norton and there is extensive written proof of a settlement. Sweyn Forkbeard was the king of Norway, England and Denmark. He ruled England from 1013-1014 and died 1014 AD. He had two sons. One became Harold IV of Denmark and the other became King Canute of England. Yes, he was the foolish one who told the sea to advance no more and promptly got wet.

One thousand years later, on July 12th 1915 to be exact, 61, Norfolk Street, Mount Pleasant, Swansea was a typical Welsh 'three up and three down' terrace house and it was there that I saw the first light of day. The back rooms of the house and the gardens overlooked the attractive Mumbles harbour, with its glorious expanse of lovely golden sands. Tourists and day-trippers were frequently heard to say, "This is one of the best coastlines in the whole of Great Britain!"

They were absolutely right!

Mum had a difficult delivery when I was born into 'the Land of Song', and I created quite an inharmonious noise. Mum and Dad had already suffered the loss of two baby sons before I arrived on the scene. They were somewhat anxious

1

about me because the concerned doctor said, "I'm sorry to tell you, Mr and Mrs Jones, that your new little baby boy is not the strongest of babies."

It seems that I constantly had to bear the irritation of wearing some horrible kind of Welsh flannel patch on my chest and I absolutely loathed my daily doses of 'Scott's Emulsion', a kind of white fishy-smelling liquid substance that everyone seemed to agree was good for me. That is, everyone except me!

As soon as I was old enough, I began my education at Terrace Road School, situated at the end of the street where we lived. You would never have called me a brilliant pupil. I was what they called "a plodder" and it was said that I was "a plodder who enjoyed school", but I really don't remember being anything like that! I certainly did not pass the Eleven-plus Examinations, but I did manage to get a prized place in Glanmor Secondary School that, for some reason, was affectionately called "the cowsheds"!

Those were the days of the super black-leaded grates, zinc baths, crystal radio sets and lavatories at the bottom of the garden. We were more fortunate than most of our neighbours because our lavatory was only halfway down the garden! It was still mighty cold and draughty in winter!

Mum diligently polished our old grate and its side hobs until they could quite easily have been used as mirrors. With a kettle on the hob and a lovely welcoming fire it certainly felt and looked like 'home, sweet home'. There were no such things as showers in any house in our street. Friday night was bath night in our home and out came the old zinc tub. A few buckets of hot water were poured into it and we were away.

I recall that every Friday evening I would try to obtain some music programme on the crystal radio set that graced our living room. I have a firm conviction that crystal sets, using a "cat's whisker", were only invented to try everyone's patience! One fiddled about until a kind of projecting needle hit the right spot on what was supposed to be a piece of crystal. Any old noise that came out was a sign of high success! Every Friday, if we were fortunate, we would hear, "This is Henry Hall speaking from London" fresh from broadcasting House in the way-off capital. The dance-band music programme would end with Henry saying, (with background music), "Here's to the next time!"

Before the age of television, listening to the radio was throughout the country a highly popular pastime especially during the chilly winter evenings. The top of the pops song sung on the radio at that time was "Bye-bye Blackbird". But later on, in the early 40s, the pop song I remember, sung by pretty young Teresa Brewer went something like this:

"Put another nickel in, in the nickelodeon.
All I want is loving you and music, music, music."

In most working-class homes, smelly oil lamps provided the modest lighting and blazing coal fires provided the warmth. The coalman arrived the same day every week on the dot and emptied a sack of Welsh coal into what we called the "coalhouse". Neighbours, back then, truly were neighbours and almost anything could be borrowed from next door. Communities were closely knit and our humble street was no exception. It was quite usual to go out of one's house without even bothering to lock the door.

Andrew's small general shop on the corner was the place

3

we obtained all our groceries. In our case it had its own bakery and the bread was as good as any that I have ever tasted. I used to love going to that shop on Fridays to pay our grocery bill of around thirteen shillings. I was given a bag of cakes free! These delicacies provided our family dessert for quite a few meals. In lots of ways, those were the good old days! Dad's wages were just around forty shillings a week, which meant that, like most ordinary people, our lifestyle was very basic. Roast rabbit was a rare Christmas special!

I am so grateful to God that our humble home was a Christian home where true love prevailed. My dear Mum was only nine years of age when she heard the outstanding Welsh preacher Evan Roberts who was mightily used by God in the great Welsh Revival of 1904. It certainly made an impact upon Mum's life. Many years later, she was able to tell me that the title of the challenging sermon she heard that day was "Fishing between the tides". I cannot remember any more of it or else I might have a go at preaching it!

My tough Dad was a conductor on what was then, in the 1920s-30s, the only railway of its kind in the whole of the United Kingdom, the Swansea-to-Mumbles steam train. It was unique; every sturdy carriage was different. In its earliest days this railway could best be described as a tramway driven by steam locomotives. In 1926 they were abandoned in favour of the then modern electrically-driven trams.

I can still visualise the "toast-rack" carriages. There were no doors to these carriages; just rows and rows of a sort of bench-seating. You could see why it was called "the toast-rack", that is, if you had a reasonable imagination. Every

Swansea to Mumbles Train

other carriage, whatever its design, had an open top. As it chugged along the track, the sea was never out of view. The train would pass youngsters "on the prom" doing their handstands alongside the little model towers they built with oyster shells. Of course, they were not just doing it for the fun of it, but rather for the pennies that would be thrown down to them by the passing train passengers. I dread to think what today's Health and Safety Standards Department would have done about it!

As a child I had a favourite pretend game. For me, our stairs became the Mumbles Railway. I would don one of my Dad's old conductor's caps that was a few sizes too big for me, and taking a bundle of used tickets I'd set off to 'work' on my steam stairs train. Of course, a packed lunch was vital. Sometimes, to her absolute horror, Mum would be the only passenger!

Many times since those days I have thought about what people nowadays sometimes, rather glibly, refer to as 'the family institution'. What a wonderful and unique idea! What a marvellous institution the family concept is, with Mum, Dad, the Children and in lots of cases, the Grandchildren and even Great-grandchildren. Who on earth could have thought of it? Perhaps it was Moses? Perhaps it was Solomon, remembering all his wisdom? It could well have been that he would have been one of the very few people on earth able to have devised such an important idea. Wrong! It was neither of them, nor anyone else on earth. IT WAS GOD! The whole family plan was devised in heaven. Psalm 68:6 makes it very plain: *"God sets the solitary in families."*

That must be the very reason why satan has set out to

destroy the wonderful institution of the family! We need to be on our guard or our society is doomed.

In 1923 when I was eight years old, my Dad suffered a severe stroke and had to finish work. He was just 51 years of age. Times were hard and became even more difficult. Resourcefully, Mum had to rent out two of our rooms to a married couple. Small in stature, Mum was barely five feet tall ... with her shoes on! But God was with her. That made her tall and strong.

It was during the time of Dad's illness that some of Mum's relatives had a wonderful Christian experience. They lived in a very small town called Skewen that was just about seven miles from Swansea. Mum said that they came to know Christ in a very real life-changing way, and they made a great impact on both Mum and Dad. Their new-found faith was so strong and they were so caring that they showed something of the beauty of Jesus Christ. As a result of their witness, my parents came into a deeper spiritual experience in God, and I certainly noticed and wanted something of it too. I am convinced that even with all our modern-day planning and advertising, this kind of personal witness is still the most telling and fruitful form of evangelism

As a family we attended the Methodist Central Hall which was in the Swansea town centre. They were the days when the Band of Hope was an important weekly event in church life and it was designed especially to warn young folk of the dangers of alcohol. One of the very special attractions was the magic lantern.

My mother and father

I still remember one of the lantern shows. Slide after slide was inserted in the lantern by hand. They told the story of a family man whose life, both personal and family, was well-nigh destroyed by "the drink". At one visit to the bar he saw a bowl of cherries in handy reach. He stretched out his hand to take one and the rough voice of a barman stopped him in his tracks and yelled, "Buy your own cherries!" It was only ten or so slides later that he was shown doing what used to be called "signing the pledge". It was a pledge never to touch alcohol again. I am sure that some readers will recall their magic lantern days and even "the Band of Hope".

Male-voice choir singing is the heart-warming genre of music that traditionally flourished in Wales, the 'Land of Song'. It has always been in essence a 'home-grown' or 'church-grown' commodity. 'Calls to worship' nearly always meant the local congregations joining together in singing the Gospel. Musical accompaniment was generally quite simple. Down-to-earth sincerity and heartfelt identification with the sentiments of the songs from the singers filled the heart of the listener with genuine emotion. Over the decades of last century, I thrilled often to the rich, melodic message of the Gospel presented by the wonderful Welsh choirs and discovered even as a youth, genuine inspiration and peaceful consolation in the music of the Gospel!

I should mention that in my young days I was a staunch supporter of Swansea Town Football Club (The Swans). Almost every other Saturday would see me in my particular spot on the 'tanner bank' when the Swans were playing at home. Nowadays, if I am relaxing at home on a Saturday, I must admit that I still look out for their result. In those days, a top rated soccer player earned about £25 a week. How very different from some of the obscene footballers' salaries in the twenty-first century!

Somebody rightly said, "Forbidden fruit gets you into a bad jam." I learned the truth of that statement one sunny Sunday afternoon. I went to Sunday School as usual. The only difference was that I was wearing a brand-new blue pin-stripe suit with trendy short trousers. I always had a real taste for blackberries and one of the lads in Sunday School knew where we could get some. I needed no encouragement. He had not told me that they were in a quarry and he certainly had not told me that the quarry was surrounded by sharp barbed wire!

I got in safely enough and ate as many blackberries as I wanted. It was easy; they were there for the picking. I went away completely satisfied and with a handkerchief filled with ripe blackberries. My friend was right about them; they were big and juicy. It was now time to go back to the barbed wire. Speedily, I bent down and managed to get under the wire. The problem came when I tried to get back up. Suddenly, there was a sound of tearing cloth and when I looked at my jacket there was an inch-long tear down and an inch-long tear across.

In one second flat I lost all my desire for blackberries. It didn't bother me if I never set my eyes on another one for the rest of my life! As a matter of fact, at that moment, I hated blackberries! What did bother me was going home to face Mum, and although she was only small – she packed a powerful punch. With heart pounding, I determined that I would delay the inevitable for as long as possible. Arriving back home red-faced, I quietly sneaked into what we used to call the parlour and put my jacket on the back of a wooden chair. Looking as innocent as I could, I then went into the dining room ready for tea. That was a tragic mistake.

"Where's your jacket, Ronald?"

When Mum sternly called me "Ronald" instead of "Ronnie" I instantly knew I was in trouble. My temperature started to rise as I hesitantly stuttered, "It's in the – in the parlour Mum."

"You don't usually do things like that!" was her answer, as she made her way to the parlour to carry out her own personal inspection of the damaged jacket. When she had finished the curt inspection, she administered her special brand of domestic justice. Afterwards, I found it too painful to sit down!

It was that Sunday that I learned an important philosophical lesson about life itself. It was simply this: "There are some things in life that are not worth having at the price you have to pay for them."

I certainly had my bellyful of lovely juicy ripe blackberries, but my brand new blue pin-stripe suit was almost ruined. Mother's anger was stirred and there was the added agony of me trying to sit down comfortably!

Whilst thinking about this philosophical lesson about life, I would like to take you now on a trip to Georgetown in Guyana in the 1960s. On the north-east coast of South America, 'Guiana' was the name given the area sighted by Christopher Columbus in 1498. Following the abolition of slavery in 1834, thousands of indentured labourers were brought to Guyana to replace the slaves on the sugar cane plantations, primarily from India. The British stopped the practice in 1917. In 1963 the British agreed to grant independence to the colony. Soon after that agreement my missionary friend John MacInnes and I passed a very large field, in the middle of which there was a huge brick stack. My friend informed me, "That stack remains there because it gives better direction to the sailors than does our lighthouse."

But there is a lot more to his story than that bit of enlightenment. John continued, "The builders of the stack feared there would be serious accidents and took all the necessary precautions in construction. Fortunately there was not one single accident. The job was completed and the workmen started on their way home.

"The foreman felt in his jacket pocket. It was missing! He simply couldn't manage without it. He just had to return to the stack. If necessary, he needed to get back to the top and see if the missing item was there. Sure, it was. It was a tough climb up the ladder but his half clay pipe was safe. He couldn't do without his tobacco smokes. He must have just about got that half clay pipe in his hand, and then it happened. Nobody knew how, although speculation was rife at the time. Did his foot slip? Was it a heart attack? Down he crashed and all around his body there were splintered remains of a half clay pipe. It had cost him his life."

Most surely, there are some things in life that are not worth having at the price you have to pay for them. In the New Testament, Judas – the traitor – found the price too high when he flung to the ground the thirty pieces of silver that he had received for betraying Jesus. He shouted, *"I have betrayed innocent blood!"* He then went out and hanged himself.

Back to my boyhood days, I saw in my Mum a selfless devotion to Dad and also a loving care for me that had a tremendous influence on my life in those formative years. My Dad was very fond of smoking his pipe and one of my tasks every week was to go to the corner shop with elevenpence for one ounce of St. Julian's tobacco.

One day he said to me, "Ronnie, you don't have to go to the shop for my tobacco any more."

Beaming with delight he explained, "I know that before very long I will have to go and meet my Lord and I don't want to meet Him with nicotine on my lips and on my fingers."

He never smoked again. A complete change came over his life. I couldn't understand it as a boy but I now know that it was God moving in his life and my life. It was around that same time that I too wanted Christ to have charge of my life. During those last days on earth, Dad just wanted to be a witness for His Saviour, Jesus Christ.

He was in one of the back bedrooms when one day he said to Mum, "Agnes, will you please make arrangements for me to be moved to the front bedroom. I just want to sing about the Wondrous Cross. Perhaps somebody passing by will hear the words and want to know more about Jesus."

His wish was speedily carried out. Day after day, Dad would sing 'The Old Rugged Cross' that in those days was a fairly new Salvation Army hymn. My Dad went to be with the Lord when I was fifteen years old and he was just 58 years of age. I am sure that he had a warm welcome the very moment he arrived in heaven.

Dad's death was a shattering blow to Mum and me. I well remember standing outside his bedroom door during his very last moments on earth. I found it hard to believe what I was hearing. In memory, I can still see the landing at the top of the stairs. The brown painted bedroom door was slightly ajar. Dad was praying in a very feeble voice, "Lord bless our Ronald, fill him with Your Holy Spirit and make him a servant of Yours!"

I believe God heard that simple yet fervent prayer. Years later a magazine commenting on that momentous prayer wrote, *"Lifelong ministry follows father's deathbed prayer."*

Yes, that wonderful prayer has lived with me and inspired me ever since. I wonder sometimes whether my Dad has seen something of its fulfilment. I love to think that he has!

After Dad's passing, it was just Mum and me. Our weekly house rent was ten shillings and sixpence. One Sunday evening, Mum said to me, "Ronnie, we don't have the rent for tomorrow ... we need to pray."

Back then I was not impressed with the idea. I thought that one had to go to work to be able to pay rent; but when Mum said "pray", pray we did. Monday morning came and just inside the front door on the doormat was a buff envelope. There was no stamp on it. To the best of my memory, there was no name on it. Inside, the only contents were ten shillings and sixpence. There are those who will say that it was a lovely coincidence! However, someone else rightly said, "A coincidence is simply God working a miracle incognito."

To me, that event was something very remarkable. It was a wonderful miracle in answer to Mum's prayer ... and I suppose I had a little part in that prayer too. I like to think that I did.

CHAPTER TWO

The Call

When I was fifteen years of age in 1930, not long after my Dad had gone to be with Christ Jesus, His Lord, I started work in the Swansea Gas Works. The first gasometer and works were erected, on Corporation land at Dyfatty and commenced the supply of gas in 1821 when the streets of the town were first lit by gas. A new gas works was erected around 1840-42 at Burrows Field alongside the Oystermouth road and that was also the site of the main offices where I began my Gas Works career.

My weekly wage was ten shillings and sixpence. I started as post boy. It was my job to pick up the company post from the local general post office first thing every morning and then sort out the letters for the various departments. I have to admit that more than once, a department received a letter that should have most certainly gone to another department!

When they moved me on to be the telephone operator, I hated it. Just to look at that switchboard contraption frightened me to death! When it came to putting the right plug in the correct hole I misfired quite a few times! More than once I was ticked off in no uncertain terms, with a few choice and angry words thrown in! The trouble was and still is that there are some people around who expect one to be perfect at everything all the time! They must have been greatly disappointed in me.

I enjoyed playing for the Gas Works cricket and rugby teams. I am quite proud to say that I captained the cricket team for three seasons, but I am somewhat ashamed to let it be known that our rugby team went through a whole season without winning a game! I cannot say with any certainty that we scored a try! The cricket team did improve on that dismal record, however, and I am eternally grateful that I was captain of the cricket team rather than the rugby team.

In later years I played cricket for the Bristol schoolmasters 'second eleven' and captained them for eight seasons. We managed to go through two of those seasons without losing a match.

There is one game that will always stand out in my mind. It was in a season when we were not doing quite so well. I am sure you will understand why when I tell you that in the Monday *Bristol Evening Post* a headline read:

REV RON TAKES 9 WICKETS FOR 12 RUNS – AND HIS SIDE LOST!

I played my last game of cricket when I was 72 years of age, three months after having a right hip replacement. During that game I was fielding in the slips. The ball came off the edge of the bat rather quickly. I dived for it rather slowly and completely missed it. When I scrambled to my feet, I realised that I had landed on my replacement hip. I decided that it was time to call it a day!

It was in 1936 that Reverend Watkin Williams, my pastor at the Swansea Methodist Central Hall, went to be with the

Lord. He was a great man of God and preached the simple Gospel message with great clarity and much power. I heard him preach on the Sunday evening and still remember one of the things he said in his sermon: "I believe that it would be God's plan that at the close of our days on earth it should be just like a ripe apple falling off a tree."

When I opened my *Swansea Evening Post* on the following Tuesday evening it told of his passing into eternity on the Monday. For me his passing was a shattering blow, because he had been such an encouragement to me. It was he who arranged for my first preaching engagement when I was just eighteen years old. As the old song says, "Ah, I remember it well!"

That evening I chose five long hymns, had a prayer time and a very long Bible reading. I preached on *'How long halt you between two opinions? If the Lord be God, serve Him. If Baal be God, then serve him!'* The whole service was over in fifty minutes. I was never asked back! I wonder why? I can well imagine someone saying, "I wish he was like that now!"

In my teen years, we held a 'Churches Together' open-air witness from time to time in the bandstand on the recreation ground next to the famous St. Helens Rugby Ground in Swansea. On one occasion I was asked to read the scripture when I was just fourteen years old. I cannot remember what I had to read but I have never forgotten the following Sunday. An elderly godly lady, Mrs Howells, gave me a Bible. She said, "I'm giving you this Bible for reading so well."

I already had a hardback Bible but this was different. It was leather and on the very first page she had written a scripture: *"I can do all things through Christ who strengthens me.*" (Philippians 4:13) I have never forgotten that truth and many times during my ministry God has encouraged me by reminding me of it.

Not long after the death of my pastor, Watkin Williams, the local town council requisitioned our church building, as they were planning street widening. To me, it was a great tragedy. Eventually I found a new spiritual home in the Full Gospel Church in Swansea where a young man – the Reverend Arthur Boston – became my pastor. We also became great friends. He records the first time that I entered his church like this: "Ron walked in with an air of 'let's see what this is all about'. He had on a grey-coloured coat which had a belt. Both ends of the purple belt were tucked in his pocket, as were his hands. He stayed for the evening service but we didn't see him again for many weeks. I was glad when he returned to the church because I felt sure that he would be a great asset to the work and witness of our church."

Arthur Boston was a great encouragement to me in every way. He gave me some prized opportunities to preach. At the same time, he told me how *not* to preach! I will always be grateful to God for bringing him into my life.

When I was 23 years of age I felt the call of God to the ministry more strongly than ever. I was very mindful of my Dad's prophetic prayer. "Lord bless our Ronald! Fill him with Your Spirit and make him a servant of Yours!"

Preparing for the church ministry would mean me leaving the gas works and going to Bible College. But there was my widowed Mum to be considered. I recall the Sunday night that I knelt down by that old black-leaded grate and asked

God to show me what to do. I was desperate to hear from God but nothing was genuinely happening. My frustration increased. It must have been almost 2 o'clock in the early hours of the morning when I did something that I have always advised people never to do. I just let my Bible fall open. My eyes looked down for some words of guidance from God. There they were:

"You are my servant. I have chosen you, and have not cast you away. Fear not, for I am with you. Be not dismayed, for I am your God. I will strengthen you, yes, I will help you. I will uphold you with my righteous right hand" (Isaiah 41: 9-10).

Nothing could have been clearer. Here, most surely, was the answer to my Dad's deathbed prayer, "Lord make Ron a servant of Yours!"

Immediately the devil (or someone working for him) brought three problems into my mind. 'Problem number one' came in a devilish voice that said, "What about your widowed mother?" The same hideous voice whispered 'Problem number two': "Where will you get the cash for college?" 'Problem number three' followed, but this time it was of a different type.

Just the previous week, I received the offer of promotion to be a salesman in the gas works showroom. They wanted my answer by the next Monday morning. On the Monday morning, I went into the secretary's office, not to accept promotion but to hand in my notice. I did so in the firm belief that God had shown me what His plan was for my life. My Mum was happy with my decision although it meant leaving her on her own. She most surely felt it was God calling me.

Within two months, I was in Bible College in Hampstead, London. In another two months, I was assigned to my first church, and in a little more than another two months my Mum had left nightly-bombed Swansea and was with me in my new little church. One can talk about the speed of promotion in the gas works, but the speed of these latter events far surpassed anything I had ever known before. I must be one of the few ministers to go to a church after just one term in college. God certainly gets a fast move on when He feels He needs to!

My first church appointment was in Ball Green, a small village on the outskirts of Stoke-on-Trent in middle England. Everybody in the village seemed to know everybody else. It was a miserable grey day in September when I left London, dressed in my smart 'Weaver to Wearer' thirty shilling suit. My shiny hair was well greased with Brylcreem. My college friend, Ted Jarvis, came to see me off from the capital's rail station.

On the Saturday night, the hall in Ball Green was jam-packed for a very special Welcome Rally. I felt my Welsh fire burning in my bones and the Holy Spirit's anointing on my heart. I simply couldn't wait for Sunday morning to come. It did come and I was in for a shock that almost made me wish I was going back to work at the gas works on the Monday morning! No packed hall. Just about the whole crowd who had been there on Saturday night were probably singing in thanksgiving and praise, "With gladness we worship" in their own well-attended churches.

I meanwhile looked out on my massive congregation of TWO ... yes, *two* ... husband and wife! The husband had his back to me, as he was playing our little harmonium. Since then I have always been encouraged that at the very next service, the Sunday evening, the congregation had increased by 100%. Our number rose to four!

For a weekly salary, I was to have what was left over after we paid the five shillings per week rent for the scruffy old hall we used for our services. The leftovers came to three shillings and eightpence. My landlady was a lovely elderly Christian lady who, in spite of her three score years and ten, was very energetic. She enjoyed a good sense of humour and she treated me just like a son.

I still fondly remember Mrs Williams for two things. Firstly, I recall her great kindness to me, and, secondly her amazing 'cottage-loaf' hairstyle. One small bun sat neatly on the top of a much larger bun. I am certain that she has long since received her eternal reward. She most certainly became part of the ministry of this young man struggling to come to terms with what the ministry was all about.

It was thankfully true that I only had to pay sixteen shillings a week for board and lodgings but even sixteen shillings was a bit of a problem when one only had three shillings and eightpence! I began to feel that those who told me I should have stayed in the gas works were right.

Then Thursday morning came and *something remarkable happened.* There was a letter with a Northampton postmark. *Who could be the sender?* I had never been to Northampton. I knew no one in Northampton. I opened it and there was no letter in it. There was just a postal order for one pound (= twenty shillings)! That event happened, without fail, every Thursday morning for just over three months.

By the end of three months we experienced the blessing of God in such a wonderful way that the congregation had increased to over 60. At that stage, we appointed a church secretary and treasurer. They decided that I should no longer just receive expenses but rather have a proper salary of £2 per week! I must tell you I have not had a brass farthing from Northampton from that day to this! In anybody's book, and most certainly in mine, that was a miracle from God!

There was a great man-of-God in a nearby church. William Scott took me under his wing. He had me to preach every Thursday over a period of three months at his Bible study even though I was no Bible teacher or much of a preacher. It was all part of God's marvellous provision!

The rear part of the church hall in Ball Green was rented and manned by the local fire fighters. God surely must have a sense of humour. There was I, trying like mad to get some fire going in the front part of the hall while they were sitting in their room at the back of the building waiting to put out the very first sign of any tiny spark of fire!

At the end of that first six months in my ministry in Ball Green, I felt that God had graciously shown me that He had indeed called me to be His servant. He proved to me, yet again, that He always keeps His word whether it is to me or to you (the reader).

Whilst still at Ball Green I met Mrs Chapman, a widow who lived in a smallish house in the village. She was left with her one little son called Freddie. At the time Freddie was just about eighteen months old. I remember the first time I visited their home. I had not met Freddie previously, although his Mum had been to the services twice. Before going any further let me tell you a little more of my new clerical grey thirty-shilling suit I had bought. I had decided on what they used to call 'clerical grey' because it seemed ideal and dignified for church services, weddings and funerals. I was wearing the suit when I visited the Chapmans' home.

There was no problem until I saw little Freddie's dirty hands. He looked as if he had given up on the whole idea of sandcastles and decided on mudcastles. Even that was okay until he started walking, as best he could, towards me.

His mother said, "Pastor, little Freddie likes you!" It got worse as he continued his journey towards me. "Pastor, little Freddie wants to come to you."

I thought about my new thirty-shilling suit and then looked at his mudcastle hands and wished with my whole being that he had *not* wanted to come to me. I could foresee tragedy looming. On he came. His hands seemed bigger. "Pastor, I think little Freddie wants to come to you and kiss you. He doesn't want to do that to everybody."

I thought, "Then why choose me?"

I could do nothing except submit. He did seem to love me. He then put his arms around me. He then kissed me. Freddie's hands were that much cleaner after our encounter but my thirty-shilling suit looked as if it had been cleaning up mudcastles!

Years later, Kath and I had three super daughters and I played and romped with them when they were Freddie's age

24

and long after. I have five lovely grandchildren and love playing with them almost any old game they choose. Humorously, I recall that I could have loved little Freddie and romped with him if only he had been washed!

When thinking about the incident and pondering the Love of Jesus for dirty old me (in contrast to God's purity), I remembered that lovely truth in Revelation 1: 5,6:

> *"Unto Him who has loved us and washed us*
> *from our sins in His own blood, ... to Him be glory*
> *and dominion for ever and ever!"*

I see the truth now! I could have loved little Freddie if only he had been washed, but Jesus loved me *before* I was washed! The poet, Charles Wesley, must have felt this when he wrote:

> *Amazing love! How can it be*
> *That thou my God shouldst die for me?*

The scripture is certainly right in declaring that when we were still in our sins, *"Christ died for the ungodly"*.

CHAPTER 3

Make me a Real Christian

I cannot leave the story of my first church at Ball Green without telling about 'the Big Joe Hassell Miracle'. Mrs Hassell was a lovely lady, just around five feet tall but she was a tremendous encouragement to me in those early days. She was probably one of the first persons to come to the church after the initial rather discouraging poorly attended services. Her husband, Joe, was a well-known character in the village. He was a notorious drunkard and his language was foul. It was said by some of the villagers that Joe Hassell could swear for ten minutes without repeating himself. He was also an obsessive gambler. His long-suffering wife once told me with tears in her eyes, "I dare not leave the rent or any other money around because Joe will take it to satisfy his gambling and drinking cravings."

Joe was usually dishevelled and walked with two crutches. One would certainly not wish to stumble across him in the dark. Despite Joe's behaviour and appearance, God's eyes were upon him for good. He was to be the very man whom God would use to be an outstanding spiritual support to me in those early months of my ministry. His witness and miraculous change of life made a great impact in the village.

I still remember the evening (a Wednesday) when Joe came tottering into the church, banging open the front doors in the process. He appeared to me to be a physical wreck and as I saw him sitting there I thought to myself, "If any man anywhere has the very clear marks of sin on his face and in his body this man does!"

Immediately after the service, he went out as noisily as he had come in. I am pretty sure it was back up to the pub for him. This event was in my first few weeks in the church since leaving college. When I told Mrs Hassell that I would visit Joe the next day, she sounded out a warning to me: "I don't know what sort of reception you'll receive. I wouldn't be surprised if he did not even let you in the house. More than likely, he'll use some of his choice words."

After that warning note, I was rather surprised when I arrived, that he was actually in. He even invited me in. He was prepared to talk. Quite unashamedly, almost as soon as he let me in, he bluntly blurted out, "I want to let you know, young man, that I have always preferred a good fight to a good dinner!"

He certainly looked as if he had been involved in a good number of fights and his appearance caused me to believe that he lost quite a number of them! Perhaps that was one of the reasons Joe had spent a good few nights in the gutter, too drunk to do anything else. I must confess I was more than a little surprised when he admitted to me, "I attended the Salvation Army when I was a boy."

He certainly looked as if that was a long, long time ago! Remarkably, he was happy for me to pray with him. When I told him how delighted I was to see him in church the previous evening, he simply said in his own particular brogue, "I'll be coming again, young man!"

As I left his home with his "I'll be coming again, young

27

man" ringing in my ears, I pondered whether his statement was a threat or a promise! Getting home, I prepared the best Gospel message I possibly could, ready for Joe's appearance on the Sunday.

To my surprise, there was no Joe on that first Sabbath! On the next Wednesday evening, however, the church door banged open and in came Joe. I was struggling through a series of Bible studies on Exodus and it was tough going, but the Holy Spirit was present and at the end of the message Joe's rough voice rang out through the scruffy rented hall, "Young man, come over here and pray with me. I can't get up off my seat!"

I still remember that night that I prayed with Joe. He interrupted my prayer and cried out, "Ask God to make a good job of me!"

God certainly did. At the top of the village where Joe's little gang used to regularly meet outside the pub, they started laying bets as to how long Joe would keep up this religious stuff. Joe told me afterwards that on his way to the meeting he called in the pub. Leaving tenpence with the barman for a pint, he told him, "I'm going down to yon mission hall and I'll have my pint when I come back."

Joe Hassell never went back! He was at the morning communion service on the following Sunday praising the Lord at the top of his voice. I remember that when I came to the time in the communion service where I quoted the words of the Apostle Paul to *"do this in remembrance of me. Drink ye all of this"*, Joe did just that! He drank the lot! Someone had to dash home and get some Ribena for the rest of us. I have always been very careful about that particular phrase ever since!

I must confess that I was somewhat reticent when Joe Hassell asked to be baptised in water because he was so very badly crippled. I could not refuse. It was a terrific service. When Joe made his way up out of the water, his face was alight with real joy and Jesus Christ filled him with His Holy Spirit there and then.

We had reached about fifty members when the outstanding evangelist Smith Wigglesworth came to Burslem, a pottery village about three miles from Ball Green. Smith Wigglesworth was one of the well-known characters of his day and today is a legend. He had no wonderful educated vocabulary. Indeed, he certainly had no great command of correct English, but he manifested the power of God in amazing ways. Via his ministry, people came to faith in Christ by the crowdful. Many were miraculously healed by God in answer to prayer.

Remarkably, an unimpressive man by the world's standards, he was born to a lowly family in Menston, England in 1859. A plumber by trade, he gave his life to the Lord Jesus at eight years of age. Called the "Apostle of Faith", his ministry was characterised by his unwavering faith in God. He was able to believe for the impossible, and yet his one main concern was that God should always get the glory and not himself.

Pastor Wigglesworth was conducting what was advertised as an 'Evangelistic and Divine Healing Crusade' in Burslem. Some forty of us, including Joe, went to a service on the local bus. The hall was packed, but nevertheless Joe Hassell struggled to the front for prayer.

Smith Wigglesworth prayed for him and Joe immediately discarded his crutches and began to walk without them. It was certainly a miracle of Divine healing in answer to prayer. Forty happy people returned to Ball Green that night, not by bus, but walking the three miles in procession with Joe and me in front. He was carrying one crutch on his shoulder and I was carrying the other on mine! God certainly did something remarkable and miraculous that night. Joe Hassell never needed crutches again!

I thank God that I ever had the privilege of meeting the charismatic Smith Wigglesworth at that time. Later I was thrilled when he came as a guest speaker to one of the churches where I was the pastor. God used him in a very powerful way. He never once claimed any glory for any miracle of healing. On one occasion he said, "God has spoken to me and told me 'Wigglesworth, I am going to burn you up until there is no more Wigglesworth left, then only Jesus will be seen'."

Someone once asked him, "Do you spend long times in prayer?"

His wise reply was speedy, "I don't very often spend more than a half an hour in prayer at one time. But I never go more than half an hour without praying."

I am convinced that Smith Wigglesworth had learned the secret of seeing 'earth's circumstances' from heaven's standpoint. What a great place to be! After many years of faithful service, and a ministry that saw the sick healed, the dead raised and the captives set free, Smith himself passed on in 1949. Appropriately, he died in a church.

I was at Ball Green just eighteen months and they were

great days ... that is, after the initial low attendance shock! The Lord taught me many lessons in those early days that I have never forgotten.

South Kirkby was not very much more than a large mining village in Yorkshire. It was completely different from Ball Green. According to the Domesday book of 1086, the records show that South Kirkby at that time was no more than small farmsteads. The village remained small agricultural communities for centuries and its farming changed little from its Saxon origins right up to the beginning of the Industrial Revolution.

When South Kirkby colliery opened, the population grew rapidly. Collieries provided the employment lifeblood, and as the pits flourished so did the town. Estates were built, as were schools, services and other small businesses, to sustain the ever-growing population.

To my delight, the South Kirkby congregation had a super church building which would seat around one hundred and fifty people. They also already had a congregation of thirty-five firmly committed Bible-based members. The previous pastor, Sister Elizabeth Hyde, made sure of that. She had pastored the church for at least eighteen months. They had prayed fervently during the whole period of her ministry that God would move in such a way that new people would come in, hear the Gospel message and would then commit their lives to Christ.

How I became the pastor, I cannot really remember! Was I invited there for a trial weekend? Was I asked to go for an interview with the church board? Or was I just invited

31

without either? Your guess is as good as mine. I think it must have been a combination of the first two.

As soon as I arrived, I realised that I had come to a local church with a very strong spiritual foundation. Prayer and the 'Word of God' were the vital pillars. It must have been a shock to their system when this young rookie pastor arrived. Mum was still with me and was a tremendous encouragement to me. I have never heard anyone read Revelation chapter five the way she used to read it.

I fully expected those first few Sunday services to be testing ones. How would I be received? Would my style of ministry be acceptable? I need not have worried, for God helped me in a wonderful way on my very first Sunday. There were some new people in attendance. I am sure that some of them must have come out of curiosity just to see what the new young pastor in the town was like.

Included in the new folk were Joe and Bessie Smart. I decided that my first visit the following week would be to their home. Those were the days when the pastor's visits were a vital part of his ministry. I had difficulty in getting in because they knew it was me! I knocked on the front door and then the back door. I did make a bit of a nuisance of myself, and after a fairly lengthy period, I was finally in their lounge.

To say the atmosphere was a little strained would be an understatement. Eventually, we chatted and Bessie said with tongue in cheek, "We did enjoy the service on Sunday evening."

Joe very quickly added, "But we will not be coming again!"

He then listed their weekly activities: "We have a couple of nights out dancing, a couple of nights at the cinema and then we spend a couple of nights at the local bingo hall."

Joe was very definite that their main reason for deciding that they would not be coming again was because it would be impossible to give up all those 'pleasures'. Rightly or wrongly, I said, "Joe, have I said anything about giving them up?"

After quite a bit of thought he replied, "No you haven't!"

We prayed and I left.

On the next Sunday evening I preached on 'What makes a real Christian?' Immediately the message had finished, a fine-looking, dark-haired young man stood to his feet. With tears running down his cheeks, he cried out, "Oh Lord, please make me a real Christian!"

Minutes later, his wife stood up by his side making the same cry to God for His mercy. They were Joe and Bessie Smart. From that very moment, Joe and Bessie never looked back in their Christian experience, and people in the village noticed the dramatic change in their lifestyle. The whole atmosphere in the church was charged with a spirit of revival. Across on the other side of the congregation, an older lady also stood up with her own urgent plea to the Lord. "Master, *please* make me a real Christian!"

That was just the beginning. Under the Hand of God the work grew. Men, women and young people came to faith in Christ. Soon our Sunday evening congregation was around ninety people. I was well aware of the fact that what was happening was, in a large part, due to the sincere prayers of Sister Elizabeth Hyde and the band of very godly people she had drawn around her. The Bible is very correct when it says that 'one sows and another reaps'. I was privileged to do some of the reaping, but of this one thing I am sure: Elizabeth Hyde's eternal reward for her service to the Kingdom will be tremendous.

It was my farewell Sunday service. A very lovely elderly sister, Mrs Evans, was chosen to give me my farewell gift. They had collected £17. In those far-off days, this was an excellent gift. She then told the story of the pastor of whom the church was a little tired. When he announced that he was leaving, the members of the congregation were so relieved that they gave him an excellent farewell gift. Greatly impressed, when he made his short thank-you speech after receiving the gift he simply said, "I didn't think you appreciated me so much; I now feel that I must stay with you!"

The pastor who took over from me at South Kirkby was Brother Jim Pears who sadly suffered from a bad health condition. Following him was Brother Selwyn Hughes, whose worldwide ministry through 'Every Day With Jesus' – the daily Bible readings – has brought blessing and inspiration to millions of lives over the years. Selwyn and I therefore have three things in common. Firstly, although we had both already pastored a church, to some degree we cut our pastoral teeth at South Kirkby. Secondly, we both agree that our days there were some of the happiest in our ministries.

Thirdly, we are both Welsh!

When I had been at South Kirkby about sixteen months I received an invitation to pastor the church in Perth, Australia, to which three families of South Kirkby members had moved. Amongst them were Joe and Bessie Smart; but God had other plans for me that would completely change my life.

CHAPTER 4

"Please peel some potatoes"

Fleetwood was, at the time I moved there, very much a fishing town, located in north-west Lancashire, at the mouth of the River Wyre. It was on the southern shore of Morecambe Bay, the second largest bay in the United Kingdom. The old part of Fleetwood is centred around the Mount, the last in a line of sand hills, with the streets radiating outwards, reminiscent of a spider's web.

The town has experienced many ups and downs throughout its existence. Especially devastating was the grievous loss of most of its fishing fleet following the Icelandic cod wars in the 1970s and the cutbacks in fishing quotas during the 1980s and 1990s.

Fleetwood is renowned worldwide for its tram system. In 1885 it had the first tramway to be electrified in Great Britain, and until recently, Fleetwood was the only UK town where trams ran along the main street.

The Full Gospel Church had begun some fifteen years earlier than my arrival, with a tent campaign conducted by an outstanding evangelist, Reverend Fred Squire. It was estimated that during those tent meetings almost one thousand people made their commitment to Christ and there were some remarkable cases of healing in answer to prayer.

Not many readers will personally remember Pastor Smith Wigglesworth although I wrote about him in the story of Joe

Hassell's miracle. He had never been to college, but he certainly seemed to have a direct line to God and his words were words of power and authority. Some time before his encounter with Brother Wigglesworth, 'Dummy' Mair had been miraculously healed in a tent meeting and began to speak fluently ... sometimes too fluently!

Years later when I arrived at Fleetwood, he had left the church and it seemed that his spiritual life was very much in tatters. He was, at that time, making his living by guessing people's weight on Blackpool's pleasure beach. If he couldn't guess your weight within two pounds either way you got your money back. A few years later, he was smitten with gangrene. Smith Wigglesworth was visiting me for a church service.

Suddenly the swinging doors at the back of the church opened with a bang and in came Dummy Mair. He was on a kind of trolley. It was just like a small plank of wood on four wheels. Both his legs had been amputated. He came forward for prayer. I would have prayed for him, but to my utter amazement Smith Wigglesworth did not pray with him or for him. He just looked at him and said with an awesome authority, *"Go and sin no more lest a worse thing comes upon you!"* Smith Wigglesworth knew nothing about him and had never seen him before. I was staggered, and so were the whole congregation. As I listened and watched Smith Wigglesworth that evening I learned how important it was for me, as a minister of the Gospel of Christ, to know something more of the power of God at work in my own life. I firmly believe that every minister of the Gospel of Christ needs to know that very power. The last thing I did before leaving the Fleetwood church was to conduct Dummy Mair's funeral, by

37

which time he had lost both arms.

The next day, Pastor Smith took me to Blackpool for a meal. It was in a posh restaurant and it was packed. We had just about settled down at our table when he put on his pince-nez glasses. He then brought out a New Testament and read a couple of verses loudly enough for everyone in the sophisticated restaurant to hear. Smith then proceeded to pray what was one of the longest graces that I had ever heard! To say that I was embarrassed would be a great understatement. Nevertheless, we had a good meal and left the restaurant. Outside was a lad selling the local newspaper. Smith took one from him, looked for some stop-press news and then handed it back and simply said, "Thanks son! I just wanted to see how the Yorkshire cricket team were doing!"

I was even more embarrassed. But I was quite encouraged to see that this great man of God had a human side as well! I did actually buy a paper. I wanted to see how the Glamorgan team were getting on!

At Fleetwood God taught me many important and sometimes painful lessons. It was also at Fleetwood that He gave me the most wonderful life partner that anyone could ever have.

It was not long after my arrival that I was attracted to pretty Miss Kathleen Gillingham. An absolute stunner in every way with soft blue eyes, a winsome smile and, above all, she was truly committed to Christ and His service. Even in those first months when I saw her, I felt I was looking at a perfect pastor's wife! The problem was that she did not seem to be one bit attracted to me!

My Mum was able to come to Fleetwood with me but

about twelve months after our arrival she suffered a quite severe stroke. My life, to some degree, revolved around her. I needed help, and I needed it badly. I well remember planning to be on the same road as Kath would take on her way home from work. We stopped and chatted for a little while and then I popped the question. "Kath, would you be able to slip around to our house and peel some potatoes for me, please?"

I admit it was not the ideal way to start a romance but it worked! She came! A few days later I invited her to come out with me one evening. I took her to Blackpool. We had fish and chips, and she paid half! Clearly, a true romance had begun. Kath had come to a real faith in Christ in the Fred Squire crusade when she was just eleven years of age. Every day I still thank God for bringing her into my life and for the ministry that God gave us together.

Nowadays in 2005 in my apartment, I still treasure the lovely picture she gave me when my Elim Church colleagues appointed me to be their General Superintendent. The photograph was endorsed as follows:

> "I will support you in all that you do.
> I will help you in all that you need,
> I will share with you in all that you experience,
> I will encourage you in all that you try,
> I will understand you in all that is in your heart.
> I will love you in all that you are."

Kath did all that to the very end of her days. She was not only my loving and devoted wife; she was my best friend, my faithful support, and my dearest source of comfort and strength. When problems came along her wise advice and counsel was priceless to me. She had an outstanding ministry of her own and became the role model for many a young minister's wife. Our three girls will tell in glowing terms what a wonderful mother she was. We shared fifty-four wonderful and fruitful years together in the work of the Lord. I know that I would never have accomplished what may have been accomplished had it not been for her. I never cease to thank God for bringing Kathleen Gillingham into my life.

It was during the time that Kath and I were courting that my Mum passed on to her eternal home. It had always been her desire to be interred in Swansea beside my Dad, and so Kath and I made sure that her wish was fulfilled. To do so we put together our savings to cover the costs of £80. My Mum had made a great impact on my life. She was truly a godly lady in every sense of the word. She was also certainly a most loving and devoted mother. During the years that she was with me in the various churches, her spiritual contribution to the life of those churches was immense. To me, her actions portrayed Christ Jesus and I am certain she entered heaven with a warm "well done" from the Master.

It was during Mum's illness that God showed me what a 'real revelation' was. She was completely dependent on me. The stroke she suffered was a bad one and everything had to be done for her. I would go out to do a visit and then hasten back to make sure she was all right. Kath came in every evening after work to help. One day I started with bad stomach pains that slowly got worse. Kath called the elders of the church to pray with me. I wish I could say that I was immediately healed. In fact the pain got worse. The doctor was called and he immediately sent for an ambulance and I was on my way to Fleetwood Hospital.

I have never forgotten the moment when the ambulance men came to my bedroom, put me on a stretcher, flung a blanket over me and carried me down the stairs. It was then it started, like hammer blows, *"WHY? WHY WHY ... WHY? WHY WHY? ... "*

Didn't God know how ill my mother was? Didn't He know how dependent she was upon me being at home? It was just as if satan himself was saying to me, "So this is your God of love?"

At the foot of the stairs they carried me past the room where she was. As I passed that room I could hear her calling my name. Was this to be the last time we would speak together on earth? How was she going to manage? What was going to happen to her? My only source of comfort was that I knew Kath would care for her.

As the ambulance rumbled along the road to the hospital the question remained, "why?" They operated the same night. In a couple of days, when I was recovering, the hammer blows started all over again. *"WHY? WHY WHY? ... WHY? WHY WHY? ... "*

It was then that the Holy Spirit brought to my mind the tremendous truth of Hebrews 4:15 where the Apostle Paul assures us (turning the double negative of the original into the affirmative) that:

"We have a great High Priest

41

who is touched with the FEELING of our infirmity."
The wonder of the Cross hit me. The suffering; the nails; the
thorns; the bleeding back; the mockery; the agony and the cry
from parched lips, *"My God, My God, WHY ... ?"*

It was the first and only time, as far as we know, that Jesus
ever said "why" to His Father. It was the first time that
amazing fact had hit me and I saw that Christ Jesus had to
come to the place where He said "why?" so that when I came
to the place where I said "why?", He would truly be my Great
High Priest touched with the very FEELING of my situation.
He knew exactly how I felt and could meet my need.

Many times since I have shared that experience of my life
with many who were facing difficult situations, problems,
anxieties and even bereavement. The wonderful thing is that
the same truth is relevant right now. The "why?" that Jesus
cried out on the Cross is still the "why?" that causes Him to
be *"touched with the FEELING of our infirmity."*

There were times of great spiritual blessing at Fleetwood
when I felt we were on the verge of something great, but
somehow it never quite seemed to happen. Like most
churches there was a very spiritual group of people but there
was also a not quite so spiritual group. One factor that added
to the difficulty was that the less spiritual folk seemed in
some ways to be a little nicer than some of the more spiritual
ones. I decided to sort things out!

I recall walking along the lovely Fleetwood beach with a
great man of God, Pastor Fred Watson, who had been a
minister of a church in Blackburn for many years. I told him
of the situation and how I intended to sort it out. In a kindly

voice he said, "Don't do that! Just preach the love of Jesus to them and you can be sure that if that doesn't change them, your list of rules, threats and regulations certainly won't!"

He was absolutely right and over the many years since, I have seen how sound that advice was. I still believe that it is good advice for every church leader. It is amazing how the Love of Jesus can completely change lives.

It was at Fleetwood that I met Mrs Wilson who was a lady with a great vision and a burning love for orphans. She obtained some property right on the sea front and opened it as an orphanage. When I arrived at Fleetwood, there were some twenty very happy youngsters in her home. It was always a thrill to see them all come with 'Mam' to the service every Sunday evening. Every one of them called Mrs Wilson 'Mam' but, of course, there had to be rules in the orphanage. One such rule was "no football in the back yard" because of so many glass windows.

One lad, Bobby, had ginger hair, freckles and a temper. Some might say that is a rather dangerous combination. Bobby decided that such rules were not to his liking. Mam was away on business, so out to the back yard came Bobby with his football. The other youngsters reminded him in no uncertain tones, "You will be in trouble when Mam comes home!"

I can imagine his eyes flashing and his temper rapidly rising. There was a wild kick at the ball, a misdirected shot and the sound of breaking glass. The taunts of the watching youngsters did not help the situation. "We'll tell Mam when she comes home!"

That only caused his rising temper to rise even higher. In

fairness, they had warned him that they would tell, but when Mam came home, she didn't need any telling. It was all too obvious. Bobby was sent to bed with a painful bottom. The end of the day came and Mam called into his bedroom.

Gently but firmly, she said, "Bobby, you have been quite naughty today. You have been very disobedient and on top of all that you lost your temper. Now don't you think it would be a good idea if you and I knelt by the side of your bed and you asked the Lord Jesus to forgive you for being disobedient? Then ask Him to take your temper away?"

Bobby seemed to think it a good idea. He knelt down and started to pray: "Jesus, please forgive me for being disobedient today. And please take my temper away and while you're at it will you please take Mam's away as well!"

This simple and humorous incident served to remind me of the power of example and brought home to me what a vital ingredient example is in our Christian witness. I was reminded of this very same truth in a graphic way in my own home a few years later. My middle daughter Rhiannon and I had a difference of opinion. She was just seven years of age and so I most definitely had the advantage! "Go up to bed now, Rhiannon!"

She was not happy. Then came words of regret and repentance and no few tears began to flow. "I'm sorry Daddy, please forgive me Daddy, I will never be naughty again."

My reply was not very Christian. "No Rhiannon, I've finished forgiving you."

She continued to plead and the tears flowed more profusely. "No Rhiannon, no more forgiveness."

She was quick off the mark: "Jesus said you had to do it

seventy times seven and you haven't done it that many times."

She was absolutely right, but I continued my very unspiritual stance: "I don't care Rhiannon, I'm through!"

Then came the sucker-punch. She exclaimed, "All right then, if it's like that I'll go down to the City Temple and tell them that you preach one thing down there and do another thing at home!"

In less than half an hour she was downstairs eating beans and chips! It is true. Pastors, leaders, church workers and individual Christians need always to remember the importance of example in both what we do and say. We are being watched!

When I was thinking about it later, I did feel somewhat ashamed. She had implored me and pleaded with me and cried to be forgiven by me and I failed to say, "Its okay! Now I forgive you!"

I was ever so grateful that Christ Jesus had not been like that to me, and still never is!

CHAPTER 5

Land of my Fathers

It was about nine months after Mum passed away that I left Fleetwood. I was invited to the pastorate of a Church in the city of Hull and commenced my ministry there on 1st February 1948. The Port of Hull is one of the UK's leading foreign trading ports and this position is maintained by a constant programme of capital investment in the development of new facilities and services. The port's position on the north bank of the River Humber also provides a major geographical advantage for transport links into and out of the UK. As a result, the port has very strong short-sea trade links with Europe, Scandinavia and the Baltic, in addition to worldwide deep-sea services.

Hull was my first appointment to an Elim Pentecostal Church and was the opening into a new dimension of ministry. Just over two months after taking up my post in Hull, I returned to Fleetwood, where Kath and I were married. The marriage ceremony was conducted by my old pastor and friend, Arthur Boston. It was Tuesday April 20th, 1948 at nine o'clock in the morning! The church was packed. Kath certainly made a beautiful bride.

For our honeymoon we went by coach to Edinburgh. We stayed with friends of Kath who had kindly invited us. We had little money and could not have gone away on a honeymoon had they not made us welcome in their home. Kath and I greatly enjoyed viewing Edinburgh, especially busy Princes Street, the city's busiest shopping street, right

Our Wedding Day

next to Princes Street Gardens, Edinburgh Castle and the Scott Monument.

I remember how Kath and I went down to the post office to send some cards to friends at home. Accidentally, I "posted" the book of stamps with just four stamps in it. We had to wait by the post box until the postman came to collect the letters in order to get our few stamps back! We were as short of cash as that.

We returned to Hull and modestly settled in 11, Chaucer Street. It was a smallish house at the bottom of a cul-de-sac. The Church at Hull had bought it as a manse. My salary was £3 and 15 shillings per week.

The Elim church was in the centre of the city of Hull that had almost been totally destroyed by Hitler's bombers in the early 1940s. Understandably people were afraid to venture out into the city centre and so numbers were very small. It almost seemed like starting all over again. It was nearly like being back in Ball Green, apart from the fact that the Hull building was even less attractive and even scruffier.

Shortly after my arrival, the power cuts ended and people who had been unable to attend began to return to the church. The numbers increased quite quickly. New people were coming in. There was a big increase in the Sunday School attendance and in the youth work. The Sunday evening congregation speedily reached around the 90 mark. I am sure that some of the increase was due to the arrival of my lovely new bride. Their previous pastor was a bachelor! Our stay in Hull, however, was not to be a long one. It was just seven months. What was God's plan for us now?

My college friend, Ted Jarvis, and his wife Marion followed us as the pastors of the Church in Hull. The blessing of God on the Church continued unabated.

Wales, the land of my birth, is affectionately known as the 'Land of my Fathers' and always had a tug on my heart. So it was good news to hear that only six months after our marriage, we were invited to take over the leadership of a new Elim Church in Caerphilly in South Wales. Kath and I began our ministry in Caerphilly on 10th October 1948.

Caerphilly is a really superb Welsh town just about eight miles from the capital city of Cardiff. Set in the shadow of Europe's second largest castle, the Norman castle dominates the town centre. Proudly standing on a 30-acre site, Caerphilly Castle is one of the largest fortresses in Europe. Boasting a tower which 'out-leans' that of Pisa, the castle also allegedly receives visits from the infamous ghost of the Green Lady. I have been told more than once that American tourists go wild about this unique castle and its picturesque surroundings.

Caerphilly is not only famous for its castle and its cheese. Fame has also come its way because it was the birthplace of the fez-wearing comedy legend Tommy Cooper. Candles made at Gelligroes Mill and workshop were used in films such as 'Braveheart' and '101 Dalmatians' and it was at the 17th century mill that distress calls from the Titanic were first heard.

A successful tent crusade had been conducted in the castle grounds by a truly outstanding evangelist, Reverend P. S. Brewster. The weather during the Brother Brewster's Gospel Campaign was cold, wet and windy. Certainly, it was not the ideal weather for such an event in the castle grounds. The ground was a quagmire. Sand and straw had to be used in abundance. However, that did not stop hundreds of people making their way to the meetings night after night for the three weeks.

Finding accommodation for our home in Caerphilly was

difficult. There were no suitable houses for sale. Eventually, we managed to get a couple of rooms in 14, Van Road. The owners were emigrating to Australia but were not sure of the date of their departure. Kath and I had to share the house with the family. There were just two rooms available for us and our furniture. Part of the arrangement was that when we took over the house we also took over the family dog, a corgi named Peter. He was the first member of the Ron Jones' household. When eventually the owners moved to Australia, it was great to feel that at last we had our own home, even though the house belonged to the church!

The first of our three lovely daughters, Glenys, was born in Caerphilly. She was a super baby but like most babies would frequently wake up and cry in the middle of the night. Kath had to comfort Glenys and I had to go downstairs and comfort Peter who would be howling in sympathy! Glenys could virtually do what she liked with the canine but if anyone came near her pram to take a peep at her, Peter guarded her as if she was gold! Should anyone come to the pram just to take a peep at her, Peter would make his first move. He would put his front paws at the bottom of the pram. He would then, slowly but surely, make certain that admirers were completely edged away from the pram.

Of course, the house badly needed decorating. Happily, there were many kind volunteers to help. Llewellyn was one. He came around to the house one Monday afternoon to do some painting and decorating in the living room. We had a cup of tea and chatted for about half an hour. Not a problem in sight.

When Kath and I returned from visiting at about five

o'clock, not one spot of paint had been put on the wall. Llewellyn was standing in a corner of the room, paintbrush in hand and a rather strained and stressful look on his face. Our dog Peter had been on guard since Kath and I left at 2.30 pm. Llewellyn never put his foot over the threshold of 14, Van Road again! Who can blame him?

Glenys, affectionately known as Glen, gave her life to Christ when she was just eight years old and at twenty years of age went to Bible College for the requisite training to enable her to work more effectively for the Lord. She grew up to be a lovely Christian lady with a great ministry in song. To my great joy, she is serving the Lord faithfully. She is married to Paul, who also seeks to follow the Lord faithfully. Paul is a Business Administrator in the NHS Medical Services.

They were married at the Bristol City Temple on 20th December 1975. I conducted the wedding ceremony, gave Glen away to Paul and then preached the wedding message! They have a lovely home. In addition, they gave Kath and me a super grandson named Chris, who is certainly a lot cleverer than his granddad; he has a BA degree in history.

At the time when Glen was born, there was an amazing salary arrangement in our Elim Church movement. There was a ten shillings raise in salary every year, and when a new baby came along the salary went up by two shillings and sixpence per week! Big deal!

Glen was born on a Wednesday, 27th April 1949. It was my great joy to remind our church treasurer that my wages were to be increased by the two shillings and sixpence on the following Sunday. When Sunday morning came, he wanted a serious chat with me: "Pastor, I haven't made up your salary as yet but I will bring it tonight. Glenys was born on Wednesday so that will be one shilling and threepence for this first week."

This fabulous financial arrangement only went on up to the fifth child. Kath and I never reached the fifth 'two shillings and sixpence'!

We had no church building of our own in Caerphilly, and so we were grateful to be able to hold most of our services in the quaint old Welsh Twyn Chapel. Their service in Welsh was at 6.00 pm on Sunday evening and so we were able to have our service at 7.30 pm. There was a really good organ but the pews were quite hard and rather uncomfortable.

Those were the days of open-air meetings, cinema rallies and street marches of witness. Every Sunday evening we packed the chapel with some two hundred people. There were many who came to faith in Christ and now hold positions of leadership in church life.

I still recall one Saturday night open-air meeting at the end of which a tall young man wanted to speak to me. His problem was one of fear. He had been a member of a RAF bomber crew in World War II. On one occasion when they flew low over a German school, they shot and killed a number of schoolchildren. This young man now had a month-old child of his own. He was filled with fear about what might happen to his child. He asked, "Will God take revenge?"

I talked with him and we knelt in prayer in the open air. I was so glad to be able to tell him of a God who loves, cares and forgives. He seemed somewhat relieved and did make a commitment to Christ. It is still true that the devil will get you and me shackled in the chains of fear if he gets half a chance!

I had been at Caerphilly just about four weeks when I planned a series of Sunday evening topics:

> Topic number one: 'What heaven is like. And how to get in!'
> Topic number two: 'What hell is like. And how to get in!'
> Topic number three: 'It's make up your mind time!'

Sitting in the balcony were two newly weds, Roy and Maureen Brock. They both had little or no thought of God. They had only come to the service because Roy's younger sister had pleaded and pleaded with them to come. They eventually came to shut her up. They attended the service for the first message of the series. They returned for the second topic. They were there again the following Sunday and that was the night they made up their minds.

Roy raised his hand as a token that he wanted to commit his life to Christ and almost immediately Maureen did the same. The remarkable thing was that neither of them knew that the other had made such a commitment until they both made their way to the counselling room. Roy became the secretary of the church and is still an elder. Maureen has been responsible for the ladies' fellowship for many years. The Word of God is still true. *"If anyone is in Christ, he is a new creation; old things have passed away, and all things have become new."* (2 Corinthians 5: 17)

As I am writing this, I recall a quite thrilling story that was told me by a Salvation Army officer friend. It was concerning a man who spent as much time inside prison as outside. It all began with the wrong choice of friends. It led to petty thieving, then to 'breaking and entering'. At the top of his list soon were office safes and any home safes on hand. He became an expert at the latter.

Then Tom fell in love. He was only married a week when the police arrested him and it was back to prison yet again. It was a long sentence for cracking yet another safe. Predictably, the marriage broke up. Tom simply couldn't get out of the net. It was prison-sentence after prison-sentence with no wife to visit him.

Fortunately, some members of the Salvation Army visited the prison and conducted a very simple service. It was then that Tom came to faith in Christ. He explained to the officer that he would like to get married to his wife again.

"No problem," said the officer, "just give me her address and I'll go and tell her and we will make the necessary arrangements."

He replied, "Sorry sir, I don't know her address. We haven't seen each other for 26 years!"

It certainly took some time to find her, but eventually the Salvation Army did. Tom and his wife were married again under a Salvation Army flag in the north of England. Some eighteen months later the officer was in the north of England for some special Salvation Army event. Tom and his 'new wife' were in the service. The officer was in a bit of difficulty as to exactly what to ask Tom. Perhaps, "How are you settling in your new home?"

It would be a bit more difficult to ask about what job he

was doing. Who would want to employ such an ex-convict even to do the gardening? He didn't have to ask. Tom was eager to tell his story: "God has been wonderful to us. We are ever so happy and the Lord has provided me with a great job. I'm now a night security officer in a bank!"

Tom was certainly a new creature. God specialises in doing things just like that!

Whilst in Caerphilly, I was very aware of the possibility that some of those who only saw and heard me on the platform would picture me as a man difficult to approach. I was greatly relieved when I read the reply of my church secretary, Roy Brock, to an inquiring newspaper reporter:

"It is difficult sometimes to reconcile the personality of the powerful challenging man in the pulpit, with the understanding and sympathetic man that he is. He is so capable of dealing in the gentlest way with the biggest problem that any of the church members might have. Those who know him well will speedily testify that he is a very human down-to-earth person with a refreshing sense of humour."

I just trust and pray that by the Grace of God, those kind observations will have been a real part of my ministry throughout the years.

Eventually, in the latter part of 1949, after some negotiations with the Caerphilly Urban District Council, we were able to obtain a super corner site for the Elim Church. Our next problem was a financial one. We couldn't afford to employ a firm of building contractors and so we undertook to do our own building!

A Christian building foreman helped me to direct the work, as my only credential was that I knew nothing about building! When we needed a bricklayer or carpenter, we employed one. The members of the congregation, both men and women, gave many hours of voluntary labour to the project. Some turned up at the site early before going to their regular jobs. Some of the men would come straight from working at the coal face at the local mine to work on the building. During that period, Kath did most of the pastoral duties and all of the sick visiting. The building progressed rapidly.

We wanted a particular type of suspended ceiling for the church sanctuary and so we sought the advice of a professional firm. To my utter amazement, they felt it would present them with too many difficulties because of the particular shape of the walls. With the opening date fast catching up on us, we decided to do it ourselves!

The opening was planned for a Saturday afternoon in 1951 at 3 o'clock. Some of us had worked through the Friday night so that the ceiling could be completed in time for the opening ceremony. The police called in during the early hours of the morning to see what was happening because, of course, the lights were on. They shared a cup of tea with us.

We managed to finish the ceiling just one hour before Reverend J.T. Bradley (the then President of the Elim Movement) was due to officially open the building. All of us desperately needed a good wash and shave. We also badly needed to change into our nice suits!

I was bitterly disappointed that some of the helpers did

not even turn up to the opening ceremony. They told me the next day what had happened. When they arrived home – they sat down, enjoyed a cup of tea and were so tired that they fell asleep in the chair ... But our efforts with the suspended ceiling were successful!

The church building cost us only around £3,000. This was almost entirely due to the dedication and sacrifice of the marvellous group of people. I love going back to preach there from time to time. It is good to see some of the 'old faithfuls'. Even more importantly, it is good to see how God is blessing the witness of the church in the town, under the leadership of Pastor and Mrs Graham Murray.

We had our first motor car at Caerphilly. It was an old green Austin Seven. I was so excited about my prized car although it was little more than a wreck. Nevertheless, I used it to travel the short distance to the church which was certainly no more than half a mile away. I used to encourage Roy and Maureen, who lived quite near us, to travel with us to church. They maintain to this day that I only invited them so that if the Austin broke down they were on hand to push! In any case, it was their job to open the garage doors on our return from church, whatever the weather.

One rather exciting day for me was when I took Kath and Glen to Swansea to show them the house in Norfolk Street where I was born and lived for many years. I was also keen for them to see the school where I spent my early days of learning. I proudly drove them there in my green Austin Seven.

In order to get to Norfolk Street we had to travel up a

fairly steep hill called Mount Pleasant Hill. I had often travelled down the hill on my two-wheeled scooter, but this was very different. I turned left off the main road to start our journey up the hill. I took the corner rather too widely and came face-to-face with an oncoming bus. I pulled at the steering wheel as hard as I could.

I'm glad to say that I missed the bus, or was it that the bus missed me? However, slowly and surely my green car began to tilt, so slowly that it seemed like an eternity. Like in a bad movie in slow motion, it eventually came to rest on its side with a bump. There was the sound of breaking glass and the plain evidence of badly dented doors. Thank God, none of us were hurt. As far as three-year-old Glenys was concerned, it all seemed to be a matter of excitement and great fun. She just ran up and down the pavement shouting, "Daddy's car broke! Daddy's car broke!"

She was enjoying the event whilst I stood there all embarrassed as some men rushed to our help. They pushed and shoved and got the car back on its four wheels. I drove off with a face as red as a beetroot. Just thinking back to some of those early-day escapades now, almost frightens me to death!

One of my last delightful tasks was to conduct the wedding of Granville Tyler and his lovely bride, Jean. On the very next day after the wedding, I had the unenviable task of announcing to the church that the following Sunday would be the last that Kath and I would be the pastors at Caerphilly. Jean had become part of our musical team and proved to be faithful as a pianist over the years. Granville gave his life to

Christ in the early days following the tent meetings. Before that, he liked his drink and was a most enthusiastic darts player.

One Sunday evening in church, I asked Granville to publicly tell how he had become a Christian and what difference it had made to him. It was refreshing to hear him. He didn't know any religious jargon. We were spared that.

He told his story: "I went with a large crowd on a specially booked train to Cardiff. I was told it was what they called 'a rally'. This rally was held in one of Cardiff's largest halls. The speaker was the same man who was in the tent at Caerphilly. Near the end of the rally, he asked those who would like to commit their life to Christ to go to the front of the hall for prayer and some literature. He said it would help us in our Christian life. I felt I needed Christ in my life and made my way to the front. Somebody came to me and said a prayer. I don't know who it was. I went with the crowd back to the train and finally home.

"The following week, I made my nightly visit to the local pub. I had a pint in one hand and a dart in the other. It was as if a voice said to me, 'What are you doing here?'... I didn't know what the devil to do!"

That certainly wasn't religious jargon either! I felt quite hot under the collar! The church was packed. What would some of the established Christians think? Granville eventually became an elder in the church with a burning heart to reach other people with the truth of the Gospel message.

It was in those far-off days in Caerphilly that I had my very first experience of preaching in the Royal Albert Hall. I arrived home, and Kath simply said, "I have a message from Elim headquarters for you but I think you had better sit down first."

I sat down as Kath continued: "They have phoned to say that Reverend Willard Cantelon from America is unable to be in London for the Easter rally in three weeks' time and THEY WANT YOU TO TAKE HIS PLACE!"

I nearly fell off my chair with the shock! Willard Cantelon was a well-known preacher worldwide. The comparison between him and me was as wide as the proverbial ocean. I had never seen the Royal Albert Hall, apart from its ornate exterior.

The Hall that day was packed. The hymn-singing and worship times were both exhilarating. They had brought over some fine singers from Sweden for the occasion. There was a massed youth choir. Then it was my turn.

I had watched all the proceedings carefully, with great fear. I had worked hard and prepared what Kath and I thought was a reasonably good sermon. I nervously got to my feet and made my way to the rostrum. This was a good day to preach about the 'Resurrection of Christ' and I put my carefully prepared notes in place. Then something not so remarkable happened. The massive Royal Albert Hall's blinding white spotlight was switched on. My mind went completely blank. I couldn't see a congregation and, even worse, I couldn't even see my notes.

I mumbled something about "Let there be light but not too dazzling," and some in the crowd sniggered and laughed. After about thirty seconds that seemed like sixty seconds, I managed to get things together and to make it to the end of the message and – praise the Lord – there were around ninety people who made a commitment to Christ. On the next occasion, I prepared myself for the dazzling spotlight!

We were very happy in Caerphilly. The people of the church were thrilled about what was happening. We now had our own building in a prime position in the town. Our occasional Sunday evening rallies in the Workman's Cinema were always packed. *Who could ask for anything more?*

Kath and I were quite snug in our comfort zone. Always be careful about comfort zones. God has a habit of tipping us out of them!

CHAPTER 6

Bristol, Here we Come!

The black telephone rang in our home and the voice said: "Ron, would you be interested in moving to Bristol to follow a crusade that Rev. P. S. Brewster is holding in the Colston Hall?"

My reply was swift. "No, we would not be interested in moving to Bristol at all!"

Two weeks later, I was invited to visit Bristol and just go along to one of the major meetings being held in the Colston Hall. I said to Kath that there was no harm in going. The Hall, south-west England's largest concert venue, had a large crowd of people and a real sense of the presence of God in that meeting. Many people committed their life to Christ. It all seemed wonderful. The singing and the excitement were tremendous, but I went back to Caerphilly determined to stay there.

A few days later, there was a second phone call to our home with the same request, "Ron, we really would like you and Kath to reconsider moving to Bristol."

The following Sunday evening, I was still very happy to be preaching in Caerphilly. When we arrived home after the service, Kath turned the whole situation on its head. She simply said, "You realise, Ron, that we have turned down the call to Bristol without even praying about it. I've been feeling that we should find out what God wants us to do, don't you?"

She was right, as she usually was. We prayed and put out a 'fleece' like Gideon of old. We prayed together: "Lord, we know the folk in Bristol have already asked us twice about moving to Bristol and we have said 'no' twice. If they ask us a third time, we will take it that it is in Your will for us to go!"

On the following Tuesday morning we received a letter from our headquarters asking us once again to go to Bristol. We could do nothing but go! It was as simple as that. I must confess I was not in love with the idea.

Caerphilly was a lovely small Welsh town where an impact could be made through the preaching of the Gospel. Bristol held many negatives. Firstly, it was a vast major city with thousands and thousands of people. Secondly, there was no accommodation for the Jones family. Thirdly, there was no church building and not even a building site.

I had no enthusiasm for searching through a large city for a site on which to build another church. We would have to hold our meetings in any hall that we could rent in the city. That prospect did not appeal to me either. I was also well aware of the fact that it would be very difficult to raise the money necessary for building a church.

It was one of the most difficult decisions Kath and I ever had to make. Paradoxically, at the same time we felt sure that it was God's plan for us to move to Bristol. Consequently, on 31st August 1952 I was conducting my first service in the rather dirty Shepherd's Hall in Old Market, Bristol.

Bristol is the largest city in the south west of England, with a population of approximately half a million. The city lies between Somerset and Gloucestershire and has been politically administered by both counties in part at various times. However, Bristol is historically a county in its own right and is properly entitled the 'City and County of Bristol'. Nowadays, a few miles from Bristol's centre, two motorways intersect. The M4 from London to South Wales bridges the River Severn before this widens to become the Bristol Channel. The north-south M5 skirts the city at Avonmouth.

Large as the city was, there was a big problem in obtaining a house for us as a family. For over four months I went into lodgings in Bristol, while Kath and Glen remained in the church house in Caerphilly during that time. After each Sunday evening, I would make the rather long journey back to Caerphilly. There was no time-saving Severn Bridge in those days. I would stay with Kath and Glen until the Tuesday morning. Then it was back to Bristol. Back to my digs and to my house hunting. My new congregation would be expecting me in the Shepherd's Hall in Bristol. The big question now was: "What did Bristol hold for us in the plan and purpose of God?"

The crusade conducted by Brother P. S. Brewster in Bristol's Colston Hall saw hundreds of people flocking to the meetings night after night. This happened even in the hot holiday months of July and August. It had only been possible to book the hall (seating two thousand) for four weeks at that period of the year because no boxing promoter or symphony orchestra dare take the financial risk of holding events at that peak holiday time. There had been a great team of preachers in the month-long series of meetings. Some of the team also possessed outstanding musical talent. Overnight, it all came down to just Kath and me, with no musical talent!

On the final Sunday night in the Colston Hall, it was announced that the Monday night meeting, and all the following weeknights and Sunday morning meetings would continue in the Shepherd's Hall. The crowd was also informed, "Reverend Ron Jones will be your new pastor!"

The people must have thought, "Who on earth is this Jones? We have never heard of him, let alone seen him!"

To be frank and honest, the Shepherd's Hall was one of the most miserable halls I had ever seen in all my life. In addition, it was at the top of a long narrow flight of stone steps that certainly presented a difficulty for older people. This was the third unattractive hall in my first thirteen years in the ministry. It seemed as if God had them especially lined up for me, just as if He was seeking to teach me some kind of lesson. To this day I don't quite know what that lesson was!

After the first few meetings I noticed that when some of the ladies came in to a service, they opened their handbags as discreetly as possible, took out a duster and cleaned the chair before they sat down!

For our Sunday night services, we just rented any hall we could get, in any part of the city. Sometimes it was the Corn Exchange Hall. Sometimes it was the superb Victoria Rooms. There were occasions when it was the dark, dismal and dingy Empire Theatre, which has long since been demolished. They were all in different parts of the city. It was a miracle of God that we managed to keep the people together in those circumstances.

Our first baptismal service was held in the tiled and echoing Wear Public Baths. Amazingly, there were some fifty or so people wanting to be baptised by total immersion in water as a public witness of their faith in Christ. It was a big event in the city and many reporters from local and London newspapers were present. There was a large crowd amongst whom I'm sure that there were a number of curious onlookers who had turned up just to see this public spectacle.

Everything was going to plan. I had two excellent helpers. The moment then came that was a boon for the reporters and photographers who were present but it was most embarrassing for me. One of the ladies came into the water and before she could be baptised, she fainted. A couple of helpers lifted her out of the water under the vulture-like camera-gaze of the photographers. For reporters and photographers, it was a field day.

Matters for me went from bad to worse. Baptismal candidate Mr Williams went one better ... or worse! Immediately after being baptised, he came up out of the water, shook his head like a dog, almost blinding me, and then proceeded to swim the whole length of the baths before getting out of the water!

On tenterhooks, I wondered how on earth these incidents would be reported in the national and local free press. The reporters and photographers were all very gracious. They wrote of the "courage" of the lady who got back into the water because of her "real faith". Regarding the "swimming candidate", they made something great out of his "sheer imagination". They even suggested that this might be an interesting idea for all future baptismal candidates! I must confess that I saw it in a completely different way!

The foundation of the local Elim Church in Bristol was being laid. We now had eighty members of whom fifty were baptised in water. Although we had no building of our own, God was moving in such a wonderful way that people began to see that what was happening was no flash in the pan.

Kath and I both realised that there would be many problems ahead. There would be the spiritual care of the new converts and their establishing in the faith. A plot of land would have to be found on which to build a church. There were also the great financial needs to carry through such a programme. We knew that we had to seek the face of God as never before for His guidance in the whole situation. The task ahead was certainly too big for us without His upholding hand. I can still write with full conviction: HE NEVER FAILED US.

The first Sunday morning communion services in the Shepherd's Hall were different and refreshing. I heard people pray in public for the very first time in their life. It was truly thrilling. I recall one of those services where I had been encouraging the folk to just pray a very short prayer of thanksgiving to God. One of the ladies, Mrs Speed, who became a faithful and loyal member over many years, simply prayed, "Thank you God for sending us such a lovely young pastor, in the name of the Father, the Son and the Holy Ghost, Amen."

There was, however, a great challenge facing us. We were paying close on £50 each week for our different meeting places in the city. That was a heavy expense at that time. There were no other suitable buildings available and no prospect of a building site. In addition to those factors, we certainly had no great financial prospects. God had to help us. We needed land and we needed money if the new converts were going to be cared for and the new church was to be established in Bristol.

It was at that time that I heard of Mr Meredith, the City Engineer. His home town was Port Talbot, a small town just about eight miles from where I was born in Swansea. I felt that the Welsh connection would make a good start to our conversation. He was most sympathetic but had nothing to offer us at that moment. I must confess that I thought that was the end of the matter as far as Mr Meredith and the City Council were concerned.

Lord, please forgive my unbelief!

Four months later I received a letter from him offering us three different sites in the city. This was it! The joy in my heart reached fever point until I saw them. They were all hopeless. The best of the sites that he offered us was in Jamaica Street. It was excellently placed in the centre of the city but it was only 30 feet wide and about 120 feet long. We would only have been able to build a monstrosity of a church on such a site. I still recall the Friday, after I had viewed the three very disappointing sites. I had said to Kath as I left the house that I was setting out on a 'safari' – hunting for buildings!

Was there a warehouse somewhere or a sports centre or a factory or even some offices that could be used for our meetings? Every estate agent I visited that black Friday said, "Sorry, no there isn't!"

It was five o'clock and by then I was miserable, weary, disappointed and fed-up. I just wanted to get home to my armchair. I knew Kath would have a good meal for me. Then it would be off to bed.

I just happened to be passing yet another estate agent's office. The office was still open. I thought, "Okay, just one more attempt."

I went in and asked the smiling estate agent the same question that I had been asking all day. "Do you happen to have anything on your books that could be converted into a hall for religious services?"

His face lit up. "I know exactly what you want, Pastor Jones. Some years ago I was part of a gospel band that played in all the kind of buildings you're looking for."

In response, my face too lit up but the light soon dimmed when he said, "I'm ever so sorry; I don't seem to have anything that would be suitable, but I will contact you should anything become available."

He kept thumbing through his books and various papers. He stopped and said, "Here's something that might be of interest, but I don't think it's much good for your purpose. It's completely the wrong shape. I've had it on my books for a long time and just can't get rid of it. It's an old L-shaped electrical component factory in Jamaica Street. It's still in production and the owner is willing to sell it for £1,100 as a going concern."

When I saw it, I came to the conclusion that it was more than a 'going concern'. One glance was sufficient to make me feel sure that it had already 'gone'!! It was in a terrible condition. But that old electrical component factory was one of God's glorious miracles. It was immediately next door to the plot of land that Mr Meredith had offered us! It was over

30 feet wide and well over 100 feet long. It fitted perfectly into the site already offered to us and made one large piece of land. God had specially reserved that factory for us even before the first hymn was sung in the first meeting in the Colston Hall! I had looked at the site with longing eyes since Mr Meredith had offered us the Jamaica Street plot and said to myself, "If only ...."

Both plots only cost us the £1,100, because we were given the council plot free. The Welsh link with the City Engineer had worked after all! God's plan for us was on the move! Something remarkable had happened yet again!

Even that was not the end. Next door to the factory was also a half-built church hall. Within a few days the minister involved in the building of that small hall contacted me. He said, "We have the option to purchase a small piece of land in a very good area where we have always wanted to build our church. We would like to buy it and could only do so if you would buy our part-built hall from us."

We bought it and the half-built building was completed in twelve months, so we began using it as our church minor hall. It was in that newly-built hall that we then held our weeknight meetings and our Sunday morning communion services.

'Elim in Bristol' was now established in Jamaica Street! By this time, we were holding our Sunday evening meetings in the Bristol Corn Exchange building on a regular basis. It truly was a super hall right in the centre of the city. It was packed every Sunday night. That is, until the winter nights came. The numbers diminished so badly that I began to wonder if we would ever get them back. But praise God, we did.

CHAPTER 7

Church Full

There were still testing times ahead and many obstacles to overcome. Nonetheless, God had miraculously undertaken thus far. We now had a truly wonderful building site in Bristol. The problem that we faced was now a financial one. The World War II years were not long over and there was much rebuilding to be done in a city that had been on the receiving end of Hitler's bombs night after night. A licence had to be obtained from the appropriate authorities before any building project could commence. Church buildings were a long way down the list of building priorities. The government had decided that only a certain sum of money could be used on church buildings each year.

I phoned the gentleman who was in charge of issuing church building licences. I explained to Mr Seath that we already had a nice minor hall in Jamaica Street and that we now needed a licence to build a church for the community. I was convinced there would soon be a licence granted to us. Not for the first time, I was wrong! His response shattered me. "I'm sorry Mr Jones but I'm afraid you are well down the list and I cannot promise you a licence for another three years. The allocation for the current year has been made. There's still a long waiting list."

Shattered dreams yet again! Miraculously, however, just two months later Mr Seath phoned me and said, "I think I have some good news for you. One church that was given a building licence for £20,000 couldn't go ahead with their plans. If my committee cannot make use of it by the end of next month we will lose it. We're not allowed to carry it over to the next year's allocation. I have offered it to all the other churches on the waiting list but none of them are in a financial position to use it at the present time. Would you be prepared to accept it?"

Accept it we did. It was a big step of faith. We, like the other churches in the city, were in no financial position to go ahead and build! Mr Seath's council committee was not giving us the money to build. They were simply giving us a licence to permit us to build. We had to find the money, and we had to find it quickly. That was the next problem! The coffers were empty and the prospects were gloomy. Money for a church building project was difficult to obtain. There was only one way. I had to appeal to the church members for gifts and loans ... free of interest, if possible.

The response was tremendous. Both small and large gifts came in. One young lady brought three gift envelopes. One was for Kath who was still living in Caerphilly with Glenys. The second gift was for the church's general fund and the third one was for the new building project. I must confess that I opened the one for Kath first! I felt God was really at work on our behalf.

One evening, early in 1954, I was invited to the home of a recently converted married couple, Mr and Mrs Coles. We chatted for the best part of the evening. Quite suddenly Mrs Coles said, "We would like to loan some money to the church, interest free."

72

Mr Coles brought out a shoebox, which was not surprising since they owned a shoe shop. What was a surprise, however, was what was in the box! It was £2,000 in brand new £1 notes. We prayed, and I wished them "good night". I could have been seen rejoicing on my way home tightly clutching a paper bag in which was a shoebox containing £2,000 (equivalent to at least £49,000 in today's money). It found its resting place under the bed for that night.

We managed to arrange a loan of £6,000 from a lending society in Birmingham. We were then committed to find £20,000, which was a huge sum of money at that particular time. The gifts and loans kept coming in. The married couple who had already loaned £2,000 loaned us another £1,500. Yet again, the interest was free.

One day on arriving home from visiting some of the members, Kath said, "Mr and Mrs Coles would like to see you, Ron."

Was this to be the day that they needed some of the loan returned? To my great relief they wanted to loan the church another £500, interest free. £4,000 was certainly a lot of money. Kath and I did have a little anxiety in case they suddenly wanted the loan returned. I recall the day I returned home and Kath met me with the words, *"Mr and Mrs Coles would like to see you again, Ron."*

Was this the moment we had been dreading? Could it be that they needed some of the loan returned? How much would they want? I just hoped that if that was the case, we would be safely covered by the arrangement we had with our bank. I decided to go and see them immediately and face whatever was to come. Before long I was knocking at their door. It seemed an eternity before the door opened and I was ushered into their large sitting room. They talked about the services on the previous Sunday. A couple of hours went by and neither of them mentioned the loan. I was wishing they would ... for better or for worse.

It was getting late and I suggested that we have a word of prayer before I left. Mr Coles left the lounge and returned with a large envelope. In that envelope were all the receipts for the loans they had made. He unfolded the receipts and in handing them over to me, he simply said, "Pastor, God has spoken to us. Here are all the receipts. The £4,000 is now a gift!"

We were still holding our weeknight meetings and Sunday morning services in the newly-built minor hall. Our Sunday evening services were still taking place in the Corn Exchange. The new building programme was proceeding, which meant that our days at the Corn Exchange were fast coming to an end. It must be said that there were many who were grateful to God for the Corn Exchange. It was there that they had committed their lives to Christ and found the real joy there is in knowing Him in a personal way.

When Kath's cousin and her husband, Dick, came to us for a weekend break, they came to the Corn Exchange on the Sunday evening. After I had presented the Gospel message, I invited those who wished to commit their life to Christ to come forward. To the surprise of each of them, they both came to the front of the hall. Dick returned to his office on the Fleetwood Docks on the Monday and immediately, he said, he removed the many girlie pin-ups from his office walls. His workmates were quick to note the truly dramatic change in his life.

The building of the new main church, named the City Temple, was completed. The date for the opening was settled for a Saturday in October 1954. The one factor that was not settled was how many of the folk who faithfully attended meetings in a public hall would now attend a church? It was crunch time. We were leaving a familiar environment to go into completely different surroundings; from a public hall to a church with a denominational tag.

The big day arrived. I need not have worried. It was impossible to accommodate the large crowd in the new City Temple. There had to be an overflow relay in the minor hall. From that moment on, the City Temple was packed almost every Sunday evening. People were weekly coming to faith in Christ. Many were being healed in answer to prayer and there were those who were filled with the Holy Spirit as on the day of Pentecost. There was a marked spiritual progress in the lives of many of the new converts. Some of the progress was only known by what seemed to be an accident.

On one occasion some years later, I was travelling back to Bristol from London. A Bristol lady was in the same compartment and she mentioned that she had just visited her son who was a curate in London. When I told her that I was the Minister of the City Temple in Bristol she said something quite remarkable: "Some years ago my son was very down and discouraged. Life seemed to have no meaning. One Sunday he was particularly bad. For some unknown reason, he decided to go to the City Temple that evening. It was at that very service that he committed his life to Christ."

I always looked upon our Sunday evening service in the centre of a large city as a great outreach Gospel event. We actually had the audacity to advertise it as 'the best Sunday night in town'. If there were no 'decisions for Christ' on a Sunday, I used to go home a disappointed and a worried man. I would quiz myself: Would it have been different if I had left something out or said it differently? After a few such occasions God spoke to me and rebuked me: *"Who do you think you are? Do you think you are the fruit producer?"* I have never forgotten it. It's the truth of John chapter 15 where Christ Jesus talks about the vine and the branches.

I was challenged by what God said to me. I realised as never before that I could not change even one life. That is the responsibility of the Lord Jesus. I saw too that although I might be able to make people feel uncomfortable during the sermon, it is the responsibility of the Holy Spirit to convict of 'sin, righteousness and judgment to come'. I saw in a more challenging way than ever before that it was merely my responsibility to tell them. That is still the main respons-ibility of today's Church.

It was at that time I realised that at the beginning of each day, I needed to say, "Lord, I make myself available to You today."

After such a prayer, He will do the rest. I saw that at the close of each day I needed to check up on myself to see whether I had truly made myself available to Him. That is all any of us can do. I have to confess that I have frequently failed to do so.

It was truly wonderful to see God working in the lives of hundreds of people and His kingdom being extended, and there is nothing to be compared with that, I can assure you! In one way it was exciting to go along to the City Temple Sunday evening services and see the 'CHURCH FULL' sign up. On the other hand, it spelt out a very clear message to me. It was imperative that we build a larger church. On a Sunday evening, should a family of three or four people wish to sit together in a service, they needed to be at the church by six o'clock. In some cases it meant that they had to leave their home at around 5 o'clock. That could not continue, especially in the winter months.

The *Bristol Evening Post* sent one of their newspaper reporters along to the church one Sunday evening. The feature he wrote was headed:

IRREVERENT? NO, BUT DIFFERENT!
'CHURCH FULL' SIGNS IN BRISTOL CHURCH

It was evident that the church was full, as there were even chairs in the aisles. It was something that he did not expect to see. The reporter worked out his own reasons for it being full. The newspaper story reported:

"The church was packed. The welcome was warm and everyone seemed to be enjoying it. The hymn singing was different; some of them were sung to a fox trot rhythm. The preacher, fiery Welshman, Ron Jones seemed to be enjoying himself too. At the close of the service a gracious lady, who I discovered was the minister's wife, shook hands with just about everyone with a 'Good night, God bless!' This is one church in Bristol that will have to increase its seating capacity very soon!"

We had some great characters in the Bristol church. For instance, there was 86-year-old Mr Guy. I remember one Sunday night when the principal of our Bible College, Reverend Wesley Gilpin was the guest preacher. The church platform was built as an open one with no rails or curtains. I was in the middle of making some announcements and welcoming our guest preacher when Mr Guy, seated on the end seat in the third row, shouted out in a voice he made sure everyone heard, "Pastor, will you ask that man on the platform to stop wagging his leg, it's getting on my nerves!"

To say that I was slightly embarrassed is far from the full truth. To this day I have no idea how our special guest felt. I have never had the nerve to ask him. When Mr Guy passed away and his will was read, he had left me £16 to conduct his funeral.

Years before, Kath's Dad had come to stay with us in Caerphilly and he moved with us to Bristol. In the early part of 1953, he passed away after quite a long illness. So in the early part of that year we experienced real sadness. In the latter part of the year we experienced real joy. On the 28th November 1953, our second lovely daughter, Rhiannon, was born.

Some months after her birth Kath and I noticed that Rhiannon, whom we affectionately called "Non", made no effort to stand. This caused us great concern, and our family doctor told us it was slight cerebral palsy. He arranged for us to see a consultant.

Mr Airbrook told us: "I cannot promise you that your daughter will be able to walk, and she may have to attend a special school."

Every parent will understand when I say that we prayed, and prayed, and prayed. It was a Sunday morning. Kath had gone into the minor hall with Non who was now almost two years of age. I was quite surprised when Kath returned to the main church and brought Non right to the front for prayer by the elders of the church, according to the scriptures. During the following week Non took her first steps.

'Non' went to Bognor teacher training college and eventually became the headmistress in one of the largest schools in the city of Birmingham. She now serves as a chairperson in the magistrates' court in Birmingham. Richard and Non were married on 31st October 1986. Richard is a very successful health insurance adviser. Rhiannon takes care of all the office matters and at the same time is a very caring daughter. With such achievements it might be difficult to believe the story of her early days.

On 21st August 1961 we became entitled to our third 'two shillings and sixpence' salary rise. Our third lovely daughter, Eluned, was born. Years later 'Leeny' (Eluned) and John were married in the City Temple. They now have four super children, Catherine, Jonathan, Elizabeth and Sarah. They are grandchildren that would make any granddad proud. I certainly am. John and Leeny have their own accountancy business. Leeny is an important part of the business working in the office with John, and she is also a super mum.

My daughters: Rhiannon, Glenys and Eluned

My grandchildren: Chris; Jonathan, Elizabeth, Catherine and Sarah

God certainly blessed Kath and me with a truly wonderful family, with three loving and caring daughters, and three good sons-in-law. I do thank God for them every day that I live.

From the very beginning of our ministry in Bristol, we were anxious to help with community needs as soon as it became possible. The lack of space was the great hindrance. We simply had to extend our premises, but how? There was no land available.

Our next-door neighbours were a couple of quaint elderly sisters running a shop. They seemed to sell just about everything one could ask for. They had owned the shop for as long as most people could remember. There was no chance of us getting that property.

Next to the shop was a large transport café that seemed to be a very prosperous concern. There was not much hope of getting that property either. Up the next side street was a row of terrace houses, most of them occupied by long-standing tenants. So there was not much hope of expansion there. I actually employed an estate agent to call at every one of those local houses to enquire if there was any owner who wished to sell their property. No one did, and we all felt that was that!

Around that same time in 1962, Kath and I were invited to take over the pastorate of one of our south London churches in Clapham. It was the place where our Elim movement headquarters was situated. Kath and I had been ministering in Bristol for well over ten years by this time. A new minister had already been approached about taking my place in Bristol. Humanly speaking, the invitation to London seemed like a reasonable move coming at just the right time for us. But it was certainly not God's timing.

Kath and I travelled to London to look over the Clapham church manse. We were also going to meet the church officers to discuss the final arrangements for the move to take place. Armed with our tape measure to check up on room and window sizes, we worked out how we would fit our furniture in each room. We had it all planned. Then the phone rang.

The executive council of our Elim movement was in session and wanted to see me. The chairman, Reverend E. J. Phillips said, "We have asked you to come and see us Mr Jones (there were no first name introductions in those days) in order to let you know that your move to Clapham is off."

What on earth had happened? Had I done something wrong? It seemed the church officers at Bristol had moved quickly. They had rung our headquarters and had objected to our being moved to London. It was quite difficult to go along to meet the Clapham church officers that evening and tell them that we would not be coming. It had been announced in Bristol that we would be leaving. But we were back in the City Temple on the Sunday.

We were always very happy in Bristol apart from the frustration of church space. To extend the building seemed impossible. Sometime later, when Kath and I sat down in the peace and quiet of our own home, we found time to think and we were absolutely certain that God Himself had put the stop to any move from Bristol. A few years later we were to see the reason why.

The years in Bristol came and went quickly. We had a full church and we rejoiced to see that people were committing their lives to Christ. Once again, Kath and I were in a comfort zone. Still there was no prospect on the church extension front.

Why I did it, I don't really know. I met with the church leadership team and explained to them how frustrated we felt. We were feeling that anyone else could come and do what we were doing. It seemed to be a matter of just holding a very good church together. I added, "I feel I need a new challenge."

One of the fine deacons that I was privileged to have said, "Pastor, you and Mrs Jones have been working too hard. You both need a break. We would like you to take a holiday. We're sure you'll feel different when you come back."

They prayed with me and for us. I can't remember whether we went on the holiday that year. But I do remember, however, that it was only about two months later that something quite remarkable happened.

CHAPTER 8

God Continues to Surprise us

The news about one of the church neighbours in Bristol was a surprise. Mr Smith at 15, Hillgrove Street was moving. He wanted to sell his house. Clearly, it was in a strategic position for us. There were a remarkable number of rooms. Also, the long garden backed on to the church's minor hall. I felt that here was the opportunity to have more rooms for Sunday School classes and other youth activities. I went to see him to discuss the matter. He told me, "I'm selling it for £2,200." The deal was done and we soon raised the money accordingly.

Next door to our new property was a small empty house. Everyone said that it was more of a wreck than a house. It was completely boarded up. Up until then, we were unable to find out who owned the wreck. Finally we did discover the owner. Apparently, a developer had purchased it quite some time previously but did nothing with it. Perhaps he was waiting for other properties to become available.

I was able to phone the owner and tell him what I needed his property for. I did wonder what his reaction would be when I told him it was for a church development programme. His response was quite amazing. He said, "I'll be happy to let you have it for the exact price that I gave for it, £1,000."

We never met each other. The property transaction was

completed by our respective solicitors. At the church, we were all getting more and more excited day by day. No wonder – we could clearly see the Hand of God at work.

Our Bristol church was later able to come to arrangements with two more house owners who were prepared to sell us their properties. There only remained three properties that we needed – the small shop next door, the corner transport café and quite a large plot of land at the top of the block. We discovered that the city council owned the large piece of land. We had never enquired about it previously because it seemed so isolated from the remainder of the properties. Contact was made with the necessary department of the council. The officer said, "We will send one of our valuers along."

He duly came and declared, "You can have the plot for £600."

I could hardly believe it, just £600! He must have noticed my lack of belief.

He asked, "Is that too much for you?"

I was anxious to close the deal before he had a chance to realise how cheap I thought it was! He then said, "We do know a little of the work your church is doing and they sent me along because they know I have an interest in church work. I'm the youth leader at the Mount of Olives Church and my mother-in-law came to faith in Christ in the City Temple."

There was no better valuer with whom we could have completed such a deal. Again it was left to solicitors to work out all the details and we were another plot nearer a larger, more modern building for the task God had given us as a church.

During this exciting time, Kath and I saw more and more each day why God stopped the move to Clapham. There now only remained the small shop next door to our minor hall, but the two elderly sisters were determined not to sell although they were quite friendly with us. The owner of the transport café continued, it seemed, to enjoy a successful business. From the church perspective these two properties were vital to any plans we might have for expansion. No progress could be made without gaining those two properties. *What would God do next?*

Kath and I prayed and prayed. The weeks passed so slowly. Would nothing ever move regarding the shop and the café? Previously, matters regarding the other properties had moved so quickly following our return from the holiday break we were advised to take. We settled back to our normal day-to-day ministry.

Several weeks later, it was around lunchtime when I arrived home. Kath looked excited. "Mr Davies from the transport café has phoned. He would like to speak to you." (Note: I cannot remember the owner's name so I will call him Mr Davies.)

I phoned him that very afternoon and he told me something that I already knew: "You know you will not be able to do anything about developing your church property without having my café. If a developer has it, you're finished!"

He knew he had us over a barrel. However, I don't think he realised that God was with us by the barrel! He said to me abruptly, "I want to get out of Bristol and I want to sell up. I would prefer your church to have the property rather than any developer. You can have it as it stands with all the furniture for the price I gave for it, £12,000. I'm also fairly sure that some of the present lodgers will remain with you, if you wish."

What a fantastic offer! The problem was that the church didn't have £12,000 or anywhere near it. We had to let it go. Our dream of extension was shattered unless God did something! As far as I could see it was the kind of property that any developer would speedily snap up with a view to building flats on the site, especially as there would be no planning problems. Looking back, I now feel absolutely certain that God saw to it that no developer realised what an opportunity that corner site truly presented.

A few months later Kath greeted me as I came in with: "Mr Davies has phoned and would like to speak to you."

I simply couldn't get to the phone quickly enough and dial his number. "Pastor Jones here. You wanted to speak to me?"

"Yes! I'm desperate to get out of Bristol! I hate it here! If you want my property, I'm down to £9,500."

Why hadn't a developer purchased this prime site in the centre of Bristol? It was only five minutes walk from the bus station. It must have been that God had put His 'not for sale' sign on it. I don't know what led me to say what I said next. It must have almost sounded dismissive to him: "Will you please come back to me when you are down to £4,500?"

At that point, human reasoning would have said, "No chance!" But God ....

Sometime later, I had hardly put my foot inside the door

when Kath blurted out, "Ron, Mr Davies would like to see you for a chat."

Up to now, it had always been phone calls. Now it was face to face. We met and my church treasurer came with me. Mr Davies was now willing to accept £7,500.

He said, "If you can pay £2,500 down you can pay the remaining £5,000 over two years at a small interest."

Unfortunately, yet again, we had to say to him, "Thanks for the good offer. However, we're very sorry that we can't take advantage of it."

The meeting closed with no deal.

A couple of weeks later, whilst I was out visiting, I felt God was speaking to me and giving me advice. I didn't hear an audible voice. When I arrived home I said to Kath, "I'm going to contact Mr Davies and offer him £5,000 for everything if he will let us pay £2,000 down and then £1,000 on the first of January for the following three years, interest free."

Kath thought I was crazy. However, Mr Davies and I met again. I stated my latest offer, and to my surprise, he agreed! Suddenly a brilliant idea came to me. Our Elim headquarters frequently loaned out money to churches for building schemes. They would surely loan us some.

"Mr Davies," I said, "what if we paid the whole amount to you straight away – could the figure be £4,500?"

Very reluctantly he agreed, with the comment, "You do strike a hard deal!"

After that one-to-one meeting I immediately contacted headquarters. The reply was swift and most unhelpful: "Sorry Mr Jones, we regret that we have no funds to loan out at this time."

We now had no alternative but to accept Mr Davies's selling offer of £5,000. I can't remember who paid the costs! The excitement at church and at home cannot be expressed in words. Thanksgiving to the Lord prevailed. We rented out the two available garages and kept most of the permanent lodgers. In the space of two years, we received £3,000 in rent. The vital corner café with the original asking price of £12,000 had actually cost us £2,000!

In the meantime, the two elderly sisters had passed away and left their premises to be sold. The money was to be given to a home for cats. The solicitor contacted me and we agreed a price of £850. The complete square of land was now ours! In all, we had purchased a number of buildings and various plots of land. The transactions were 28 in number! *God had worked miracle after miracle!* There are probably few ministers who have been in the property market so many times.

The question now was: *What were God's plans for the future?*

Kath and I prayed fervently that God would make His will very clear to us. In July 1969, I was convinced that God showed me how to proceed. There had to be a main building to seat at least 500 people and separate areas for different Sunday School age groups. We also needed a gallery that could easily be divided into two rooms. One soundproofed room would be for a crèche and the other for a meeting place for small groups. The plans were also to include a room especially designed for public address equipment. There was to be a private car park. Because of our vision regarding help in the community, there had to be sheltered residential accommodation for twenty senior citizens. Other offices and a minister's vestry were also part of the plan.

Kath and I kept these initial thoughts about the plan to ourselves. Had we really heard from God? Or was it all our own ideas? I felt that God needed to confirm to us if our ideas were really His plans. Clearly, such a new building was going to be very costly. We need not have worried about such matters.

On a cold evening in December 1969, our church treasurer and his wife, Bob and Mavis Helps, invited us to their home for a Christmas meal. At about 8.30 pm that same evening, Bob produced quite an amazing model of the new building. He had constructed (in model size) a large church auditorium with some little model people plus some separate areas for Sunday School and youth work. The model included a car park (with small model cars and trees) and residential accommodation for 20 senior citizens!

With a smile on his face, Bob said, "Pastor, only Mavis and I know about this. I've been working on this model for six months. I actually started the construction away back in July!"

My heart skipped a beat. Kath and I thought to ourselves, *"Confirmation indeed!"* Since it was going to involve a great deal of money for such a large building programme, Kath and I were grateful to God that He had given the same vision to the treasurer too. How marvellously God had moved!

We decided to proceed with the appointment of an architect. This was a real step of faith, for at that time our weekly offerings were about £75. We realised that we would need that to be increased to at least £700 a week to finance our new building project. Finally, the four of us knelt and prayed together.

We agreed to call the project 'Operation 1975'. Our plan was to commence construction in 1975. We felt that would be a reasonable date. God, however, had other plans and I had the joy of laying the foundation stone of the new building on 25th August 1973. God moved so miraculously that our 'Operation 75' had become His 'Operation 74'. The new completed complex was opened on 20th April 1974. It was also the date of our wedding anniversary. What a glorious day!

The following report appeared in the local paper:

AN EXCITING BUILDING

The City Temple which was opened on April 20th is quite a new concept in church building with its unique ceiling design of light wood finish, and its unusually positioned baptistry. The interior walls are mostly finished in brickwork. It is planned so as to give special teaching areas for the 300 strong Sunday school. The Sunday evening revival rally is vibrant with life. The congregation sing with sincerity and fervour to the accompaniment of Hammond organ, piano and even guitars and drums!

Mention must be made of the Memorial Hall and lounge with the simple plaque, "our tribute to the many faithful members of earlier years who have now entered their eternal reward."

April 20th was certainly a highlight in one of Bristol's most thriving churches but as its minister and members

declare,
> "The end is not yet, praise the Lord."

I cannot close the description of those thrilling days without recording one event which humbled me and which I will never forget.

Tony, our architect, was a bright young man. The very design of our new building was abundant evidence of his very modern approach to building design. The time came when we had to decide on the type of cross that we wanted outside the building. I explained to him my ideas: "Tony, I would like an attractive ornate cross outside the church. It must be floodlit, so that passers-by will see that the Cross of Christ is central in all our activities."

In a couple of weeks Tony came back to me. His words shook me rigid. I was barely prepared to consider his radical idea. "Reverend Jones, about the cross, I have decided to get two railway sleepers, bolt them together, put them in the place you wish and then have them floodlit."

"Tony," I replied, "you must be joking. That's just not possible. A couple of dirty old railway sleepers outside our super new attractive church? I want something better than that!"

Tony, however, returned a week later and he had certainly not come up with anything better. Tony was adamant. He insisted on railway sleepers. Finally, I said, "Okay Tony, I agree on certain conditions. You will plane off the rough edges and make them nice and smooth. You will varnish them before putting them in place."

"No!" he replied. "I just want to put them up as they are!"

I tried once more. "Tony, I have to tell you that I certainly do not think that railway sleepers will look nice up there."

Tony then preached me one of the most humbling and challenging messages I have ever heard. "Reverend Jones, if what you preach inside your new building is right, the cross of Jesus was not nice, was it?"

Tony was right. I was humbled. The cross of Christ was ugly and rough. The passion of Christ was horrendous. Tony's rough railway sleepers were erected and remain there to this day outside the Bristol City Temple. The truth is that the Cross of Christ must always be central to our message as the Church of Christ. If it is not, we write our own epitaph, we sound our own death knell and we dig our own grave. God forbid that this should ever happen to the Church, which is His body!

CHAPTER 9

The Church in Action

It was thrilling to watch the progress of the new Bristol City Temple building. I recall the day when the foreman invited me into his office. He was keen to show me the blueprints. He declared, "Mr Jones, these are the things that matter. As long as we keep to these blueprints you will have a smashing building!"

That was the day when God showed me something from the Bible that I have never forgotten. In Exodus chapter 24 God said to Moses, *"Come up to me in the mountain."*

Moses remained on the mountain for forty days and nights. God then said to him, "Here's the blueprint for the worship tabernacle I want you to build."

As Moses was just leaving the mountain with the plans, God's voice spoke again: "By the way Moses, don't ever forget to build according to the pattern that I have given you!"

I too heard the voice of God that day through the words of a building foreman. God has a plan for all our lives. For many of us, we might well be able to recall when He showed it to us. The big question is: What have we done about it?

I have found in life that there are many voices that clamour for my attention. God still whispers, 'remember My plan'. I wonder what would have happened to our building if the plumbers, bricklayers, carpenters, electricians (and others involved) rebelled and determined to do their own thing:

"We'll just forget the blueprint from here on and just do it our way!"

What a 'Babel' that would be! In such an event, we would have been left with some monstrosity of a building which would have been an eyesore to all who saw it. It would have been no good me blaming the architect. His drawings were clear.

I do get a little tired of those folk who glibly say that "it's all God's fault" when matters go wrong. I like to remind them that God gave us a blueprint for living. His Son, Christ Jesus delivered it in person when He came to earth. He was the One who declared, *"I am the way, the truth and the life."* I must seek to live my life in accordance with 'God's Blueprint for Living'!

Christianity – to a large extent – is 'Christ-in-action through His Church'. God needed a human body and Jesus became the body of God on earth. In chapter one of his Gospel, the Apostle John states that very truth like this: *"The word became flesh and dwelt among us. We beheld His Glory as of the only begotten of the Father, full of grace and truth."*

We know exactly what God is like because Jesus has revealed Him to us in human form. Later, the Apostle Paul reminded us that the Church is now His Body on Earth. In the same way that Christ Jesus portrayed God in all His fullness for thirty-three years on Planet Earth, so the Church must portray Jesus now by converting our faith into everyday living.

The Bristol City Temple's great opening day event, with all its excitement came and went. That chapter in the ongoing saga was now over; the hard work was about to begin. All church members agreed that it was now time for action. The afternoon Sunday School increased so quickly that we were almost taken by surprise. There was an attendance of around three hundred youngsters ranging in age from three to twelve years. A staff resource of between forty and fifty teachers was needed. The teenagers and adults had their own Bible classes. It meant that on Sunday afternoons there was an attendance of around 400. Sunday afternoon at the City Temple took on a new meaning. It was alive with action accompanied by no little noise and, of course, a few problems.

As a church, we felt that God was enlarging our vision and that an effort should be made to reach youngsters in other parts of the city of Bristol. So we commenced 'Junior Crusaders' activities in five community centres in various parts of the city. We obtained the permission of day school headteachers, to give out invitation leaflets to the children as they left schools at the close of the schools' sessions.

Reverend John Marriott was working with me at the time and it was his task to start a branch in the Co-op Hall in the Southmead area of Bristol. First of all, there had to be the distribution of the leaflets. When we met up later, I simply asked the question, "How did you get on at the school, John?"

He seemed a very weary John who replied, "How did I get on? I'll tell you exactly how I got on. I didn't give out a single leaflet. They just pinned me against the wall and took the leaflets out of my hand ... ha ... ha!"

The first session at Southmead was a great success. Between the Sunday School and the five week-night Junior

Crusader branches, we were reaching around 500 children every week. These efforts demanded a group of dedicated workers with a great heart to reach youngsters with the story of Jesus and His Love. Eventually, we hired buses to bring some of the children into the Sunday School at the church. A number of them committed their lives to Christ and became faithful members of the church.

I really did land John Marriott into a very difficult situation. We had been working together for about three months when I suggested to him that it would be good for him to conduct the funeral that was due to take place in a few days' time.

He agreed but then added, "I don't have a minister's manual."

"That's no problem John, you can borrow mine."

Unfortunately I had not erased the pencilled-in name for the previous funeral I had conducted. You can probably guess what happened! ... He did forgive me!

At the other end of the age spectrum there were the elderly and lonely to be considered. I am thankful that the assistant ministers who worked with me in this department (and in every other area of the work over the years) were excellent. Since that time, most of them have gone on to pastor flourishing churches and some to leadership positions in the Elim movement. It would not be fair to mention any names. Their part in the ministry of the City Temple was vital to the work.

One name I *must* mention, however, is Miss Winnie Collins. She retired from a very good job and wanted to work among what she called "the shut-ins". When she visited she would have a cup of tea and a chat with them. She would also go on any errands to the shops for them, including the collection of their medication from the chemist and any pension due from the post office. Her contribution to the work was outstanding and yet amazingly, she remained unpaid. She was only prepared to accept expenses. We always felt that caring for people is as much a part of the ministry as is preaching.

Christmas can be a very lonely time for some people and so, as a church, we felt we should do something about it. Plans had to be made well in advance. We would notify, through radio notices and newspaper articles, those who were living alone that they were all very welcome at the 'City Temple Christmas Dinner'. Our volunteers with cars would call on them and bring them along to the 10.30 am Christmas morning service. The minor hall was divided into two parts: the dining room and the lounge. The lounge area was very welcoming with its rugs and nice comfortable chairs. All the usual Christmas decorations – complete with a Christmas tree – were provided. These extras were brought in by church members and made half the minor hall really look like a super lounge. It was fairly easy to make the other half of the hall look like a first-class dining room. We had a group of wonderful workers who were dedicated and committed to this task.

Our young daughters, Glen, Non and Leeny were reasonably happy about the arrangements and they did play their part well in the celebrations. They received an extra Christmas Day and Boxing Day as a well-deserved reward. The menu was excellent. It included turkey with all the trimmings and, of course, Christmas pudding. After dinner it was time for a short nap for most of the guests. Everyone was awake in good time for Queen Elizabeth's Christmas TV speech in the afternoon. This was then followed by a visit from Santa Claus with presents for all. Our middle daughter, Non, was always afraid of Santa Claus, even when she knew who it was!

Sometimes even the Lord Mayor of Bristol would drop in on us. Members of the New Creation Singers from the church would give up some of their Christmas Day and come in the afternoon to sing to, and chat with, those who would otherwise have had to spend Christmas alone. There would inevitably be a good sing-along of favourite carols. Mince pies and cups of tea ended the day. The volunteer chauffeurs would then come back to drive the folk back to their home.

Without exception everyone who came expressed their grateful thanks for their Christmas treat. The number of lonely folk who came along on Christmas Day usually numbered about forty or so. Alex and Herbert Criddle, together with many others, were a tremendous help to Kath and me during this annual event. We looked on it as a very important part of the Church's ministry and well worth while.

During the 1970s, the City Temple attracted a large group of young people, and I would stay with them after the Sunday evening service for a sing-along time. It was great fun. I remember how one Sunday night one of them came up with a great idea, "Pastor, it would be good if we could sing at one of the Sunday evening services."

Thus it was that the 'New Creation Singers' was launched.

The group consisted of between seventy and eighty enthusiastic young people who made up their own harmonies as they went along. It had to be that way because their conductor didn't understand a note of music! It was me!

This was before the days of modern worship groups. God blessed us with some excellent musicians. I think we were one of the first UK churches to introduce drums into a service. We could only do it because we had a terrific drummer named Peter Standerwick. One hardly knew that he was there at times but one certainly missed him if he wasn't! I reckon that Peter is a good role model for drummers everywhere!

It was not long before the New Creation Singers were on radio and TV. The Singers also quickly came to the attention of recording companies and the first of their four album recordings on the 'Pilgrim' label, "Let's celebrate" was very soon in Christian bookshops nationwide.

The next step in my new musical career was rather more frightening. Every Easter Monday, the Elim Churches held major rallies in London's famous and historic Royal Albert Hall with congregations of at least 5,000. An important part of the great day's events was the singing of a massed youth choir of at least three hundred. The singers were drawn from many churches in every part of the United Kingdom. The conductor was a top-class musician, Douglas Gray, who for many years was the conductor of the beloved London Crusader Choir. He had planned the Royal Albert Hall songs and the musical arrangements for many years. He felt it was time to retire from that particular task and a replacement was needed. Some bright spark said, "You can do it, Ron!"

The proposal came from one of the members of the Executive Committee when members were discussing the matter. All the members reckoned that I could do it. They simply saw the success of the 'New Creation Singers' and added 2 and 2 together and made 5! Didn't they know that the success of the New Creation Singers was really due to my daughter Glenys, the musicians and the utter enthusiasm of all our young people?

I was cornered. Should I say, "Sorry, the answer is 'no' because I don't understand a note of music"? Or should I say, "Yes, I will do my best"?

I did the latter. I have wondered many times since if my 'yes' answer was due to just wanting to help or was there a bit of pride? Probably it was a mixture of both.

I did the joyous task at the Royal Albert Hall for eight years. On the final occasion, amazingly, we had a youth choir of over six hundred voices. I still love to lead a group of singers if I get half a chance. If there is no half a chance, I try my very hardest to make one although I still don't understand a note of music!

What can be said about our wonderful yearly camping week at Llanmadoc? The location was a small quaint village on the superb Gower coast just a few miles from Swansea. Llanmadoc takes its name from the Church of St Madoc. It has guesthouses, a small shop/post office with tearoom, one pub and a large number of holiday homes and camping sites. Gower peninsula is one of Britain's best holiday destinations. The first area in the United Kingdom to be designated an

Area of Outstanding Beauty. It has simply got everything: towering cliffs, sandy beaches, great watersports facilities, a fascinating history and all the benefits of a thriving city only a short drive away. Part of the charm of Gower is that it is so unspoiled. Even on the busiest bank holiday you can escape the crowds and enjoy the seclusion of your own piece of glorious golden sands.

Our camp had a couple of places that they called the "ladies' dormitories", and there were similar arrangements for the young men. It would be impossible to imagine anything less like a dormitory! The mattresses were palliasses into which the campers put their own straw, provided by the camp manager. Dormitories were each given a couple of oil lamps together with a grave warning of how careful campers needed to be. There were no flush toilets.

It must be said that accommodation and facilities did improve year by year. Nowadays there are excellent facilities. Back then, on the plus side, there was the magnificent beach that was virtually solely for our camp. There was a large field for every type of sporting game. I managed to get on the winning side most times. For some reason or other, some of the campers used to think that I cheated! As if I would!

Best of all, there was the quaint but lovely little chapel where some youngsters committed their life to Christ. Most of them went away with a greater desire for God. The camp was surrounded by majestic green hills. Quite frequently groups of the young folk would go to the hilltops early in the morning and later in the evening to pray.

Kath and her willing voluntary staff made sure that the campers were all well fed. However, on one occasion some pie or something that had been reheated caused some problems. I think they called it a "tummy upset"! The next morning came and there were some campers who kept their seat in the loo for the rest of the day! One young man was heard to say, "I'm not going to give up my seat for anyone!"

The number of young people who came each year throughout the 28 years that we had the camp averaged about eighty. Friday night at the camp was a very special night. It was our final service. A listing of the 'Top Ten' choruses of the week was announced along with various awards. One award went to the 'Hungriest Camper'. One went to the 'Laziest Camper'. One each also went to the 'Most Ladylike' and the 'Most Gentlemanly'. The top awards went to 'Mister Llanmadoc' and 'Miss Llanmadoc'. Their prizes were for the next year's camping week that was given to them entirely free.

All this was followed by a bonfire at the top of one of the hills with a happy sing-song time. A bucket containing twigs was placed not too far from the fire. Those young people who just wanted to take a new step forward in their Christian life were invited to take a twig and throw it on the fire. These were important and moving moments. Amongst those youngsters who did this over the years were some who went into full-time ministry. Philip Niblett who is now minister of a church in Hull was one that I remember. Philip had previously committed his life fully to Christ in the little camp chapel.

I well recall the night when one young lady went forward. She took her twig from the bucket and went a little closer to the fire. Mary stood there a few moments as if she was praying. She then threw the twig on the fire, and stood there a few moments longer before returning to her place in the group.

I spoke to her afterwards. "Mary, why did you come forward tonight?"

"Pastor, I just wanted to tell the Lord Jesus that I'm willing to go to the mission field for Him."

Mary Fisher went to Rhodesia in Africa and sadly was one of nine Elim missionaries and their four children who were massacred by guerrilla forces in that country in 1979. The murder was a tragic end to the life of a committed young Christian lady. But great is her reward from the Master in Heaven.

Mention must be recorded about the Bristol City Temple's vision of sheltered accommodation for senior citizens. You will recall that a large piece of land right at the top of the block was purchased and that we now owned. We built our first multi-dwelling house right there. It provided accommodation for twenty-two senior citizens plus their own on the spot warden. Further developments were to follow. Each one carried the name of one of the pioneers of Great Britain's Elim churches. We named this particular one, Hathaway House. The Bristol City Council was most helpful to us in every way. They had sold us a large plot of land for just £9,000 for this purpose and allowed us to pay back the loan in reasonable instalments. On that plot there are now two more developments. These carry the names of Phillips House with fifteen flats, and Henderson House with five flats.

A little later some more property right opposite the

church became available. In conjunction with the Elim Housing Association, it was purchased and another house was built providing accommodation for just over fifty young people. They kindly named it Ron Jones House. As a result it now meant that the Bristol City Temple had provided accommodation for well over one hundred people. Of course, this greatly pleased the Council's Housing Department for obvious reasons.

We felt that we were seeing at least part of the vision that God gave us come to fruition! It was quite exciting and yet very humbling to see God moving in such a powerful way. Often when I now meet people who were with us in the City Temple at that time, they invariably say, "Pastor Jones, those days were awesome days."

I believe they were, too.

CHAPTER 10

Reaching Out

Every conversion to Christ is eventful and is a Divine miracle. There are some, however, that seem to stand out in one's mind. My friend, Des Morton was such a one. He will tell his own story:

> "I was converted to Christ in September 1955. Some close friends of mine, Jim and Pauline Douglas, invited me to go with them to the Bristol City Temple. After several such invitations I went.
>
> As soon as I entered the large modern building, I couldn't help noticing that it was packed with hundreds of people. There were chairs down the aisles. The meeting was vibrant with singing and praise. It was alive with what I now know to have been a revival atmosphere. I saw a smart dark-haired man with spectacles take his seat on the platform. Jim turned and whispered in my ear, 'That's Pastor Jones!'
>
> That night the Reverend Ron Jones preached on the theme of the 'Cross of Christ' and entitled his sermon 'The Slain Way'. He vividly described the crucifixion of Jesus in such a dramatic way that I could almost see it. It was in that very service that I became aware of God speaking to my heart and was surprised to find myself weeping as I sat listening. When Pastor Jones invited

people to surrender their lives to Christ and receive
Him as Saviour and Lord, I found myself saying 'yes'
in my heart.

"I was soon walking down the aisle, sobbing with
tears of repentance as I went. I knelt at the
communion table and committed my life to Christ.
When I arose, I was a new man! From that moment
on my life took a completely new direction as the God
that I always knew was there, came into my life. I had
the privilege of sitting under the anointed ministry of
Pastor Ron Jones for ten years. During those years, I
grew in the things of God as He prepared me for the
work that was to come."

I recall the evening of Des' conversion so well, but I was
somewhat sceptical and rash in my conclusions. When I
arrived home that night Kath asked me, "How did you get on
with that young man tonight, dear?"

With very little enthusiasm I said, "All right, but I don't
think he will amount to much!"

How completely wrong I was! I have lived to learn how
absolutely foolish it is to make quick decisions about people
and situations.

This brings me easily to our City Temple outreach
programme. Keynsham is a small town about seven miles
from Bristol, about halfway between Bristol and Bath. To the
best of my knowledge the town has a lively market every
Friday. The Parish Church of St John has an interesting
Jacobean pulpit and a beautiful seventeenth century tower
that offers good views over the surrounding countryside. The

River Avon skirts around the edge of Keynsham and there are delightful riverside walks with country pubs and cafés. The town is also famous for its chocolate factory, which gives the town its tantalising aroma. The factory was originally owned by the Frys but is now part of the Cadbury group.

After being in Bristol a few years I felt it was time to rent a local hall and hold a series of church services in Keynsham. We were able to rent the Co-operative Hall for two weeks. The results were far from brilliant. However, the support from the home church in Bristol was tremendous and we packed the hall every evening. At the end of the two weeks, we had between 18-20 people who wanted us to establish an Elim Pentecostal church in the town. We continued to hold Sunday services in the Co-op Hall. The small group of people proved to be most faithful. My assistant-pastors from the Bristol church did their utmost to build up the work.

At the time, a Methodist church in Keynsham closed and was advertised for sale. The asking price was £2,000. We made an offer of £1,000. Not surprisingly the offer was rejected. Then, it was almost three months later that I received a letter from Manchester telling me that the offer had been accepted. The letter arrived on a Wednesday morning.

Wednesday evening was the time for our weekly well-attended Bible study at the City Temple. I announced the good news to the congregation that our offer had been accepted. There were expressions of joy and elation. I then announced, "Now friends, I have to tell you the bad news. We don't have a thousand pounds!"

The big question was: *from where were we going to get*

the £1,000? We had just bought another property in Hillgrove Street and the coffers were almost bare.

The very next day at lunchtime, something remarkable happened. The doorbell rang. Kath answered the door and invited the nicely dressed stranger in. Neither of us had ever seen him before. We stood looking at each other in silence for a few moments. It seemed like an eternity. Without any undue emotion he said, "You want to buy a chapel in Keynsham, don't you?"

I replied, "Yes, we do."

"You need £1,000, and that's what I've come to see you about. God has laid it on my heart to buy it for you."

Was I hearing right? Was he a conman who would soon want money out of me? I tried to look as thankful and believing as I could, but I was not sure. He then made this promise, "I will go and make the necessary arrangements to draw the money from my bank and I'll be back the same day next week."

Thursday came. Kath and I stayed in. We were waiting for the bell to ring. Would he come back? The bell rang. It was only the postman. It rang a little later on. It was him. He was firmly holding a little black attaché case. He opened it and handed me one thousand brand new one-pound notes. They could not have looked any better if he had specially made them himself.

When we asked him how he knew we needed that particular sum of money, he said, "All day last Wednesday, it seemed that the Lord was telling me that I had to go to the City Temple that evening, and that was why I came and that was when I heard about the need!"

Kath and I stood there in wonderment. We were now convinced that this was God moving and working a miracle. The most amazing thing was that this was the first and only time that he had ever been inside our church! He never came again. I actually invited him to the opening of the new church in Keynsham that he had bought for us. He refused the invitation. I asked, "Why did you do it then?"

His reply truly moved both of us. "I went to Sunday School in that old Methodist chapel as a boy and I don't want to see it used for anything else."

There are two very important spiritual lessons here for every one of us. They are firstly, the great faithfulness of God and secondly, the importance of our obedience to His voice with its clear direction for our lives.

The next turn of events was equally thrilling. There was an evangelistic mission hall on the estate in Keynsham. It was a corrugated building which had previously been used as the old isolation hospital. The small group of worshippers who were using it felt unable to continue.

Years earlier, the council had let them have the building and the very large piece of ground for a very small sum of money. There was, however, the stipulation that they had to demolish the old building and rebuild within ten years. The ten years had expired and the mission folk were not able to carry out the new building programme. A very godly lady contacted me and offered the property to us together with the £300 that they had saved for the building. She did, however, want to know exactly what our beliefs were before the transaction was finally settled.

I met with the small group of members who had so

faithfully kept their mission-church going over the previous year. They were happy and we were delighted to accept their kind offer. At the same time, I assured the Keynsham Council that there would be a new church constructed on that piece of ground within two years. The two-year period was just about ending when the opening ceremony of the promised new church took place to the glory of God.

Keynsham now needed a pastor with charisma, vision and the anointing of the Holy Spirit on his preaching. In addition, he would have to follow a daily job to support himself and his family. Who would be willing to tackle such a task? Where could I find such a young man? I did find one. It was Des Morton, the very same young man of whom I had said, "*I don't think he will amount to much*"! The ironic thing is that it was me who had to go and ask him to do it! God has His own way of humbling us!

In 2005 Keynsham Elim Pentecostal Church is still flourishing with a large congregation and a superb building with all the necessary facilities.* They have now made use of the whole of the site. It has a great evangelistic vision and in addition to its street ministry and its prison and hospital ministries, they have already opened two branch churches.

I am always thrilled to preach at Keynsham because I feel that, in some way it is part of the outreach of the City Temple and Des nearly always introduces me as "his pastor". Des Morton and his wife Rosalie have now been at Keynsham since 1977 and I feel sure they will never be leaving Keynsham. God certainly put them there!

Note: You can read about the miraculous provision of that building in Des Morton's book *Stepping-Stone Miracles.*

I shall never forget the church campaign that I conducted in Portsmouth. A good friend of mine, Reverend Archie Biddle, who followed me into the pastorate of the City Temple. invited us to his church. I had an excellent pianist in Neville West and a good soloist in Don Evans. Everything was going great apart from the fact that Kath had a few problems to cope with whilst I was away.

The church secretary, Alan Pinchbeck, worked in a solicitors' office. After one of the Portsmouth meetings he told me, "Some of the partners and staff from the office are coming to the service tomorrow evening."

This was great news. Sure enough they came. There was an excellent congregation. The singing was at its best. I thought I was preaching quite well. In my sermon I said something I felt sure everyone accepted as fact. I was in full flow and said with confidence, "I know there is no one here tonight who would say that they have never sinned in all their life."

Then it happened. One man, who I had never seen before, shouted out loudly enough for everyone to hear, *"I WOULD!"*

My sermon fell apart. I was embarrassed. Could this be someone from the solicitors' office? If not, what on earth would they think they had come into? I did the first thing that came into my mind. I said: "Will you please stand, sir, so that we can all see you?"

He stood, upright and unashamed. Our public conversation commenced. "Sir, are you telling me that you have never done anything wrong in the whole of your life?"

"Yes, I am," he replied.

What could I say? I repeated my question with a slight variation: "Sir, have you never said anything wrong in the whole of your life?"

"No, never!"

Things were really getting difficult now. A few seconds seemed like an eternity. I was getting hotter and hotter under the collar by the second. I could try one more question. "Sir, do you mean to tell me you have never thought anything wrong in all your life?"

"That is exactly what I'm telling you!"

I still don't know what I would have done had not God come to my rescue through the moving of His Holy Spirit. I declared, "Sir, if it is true that you have never sinned in all your life, I have to tell you that you have just committed your first one. The Bible says (1 John 1: 8,10), *'If we say we have no sin we DECEIVE OURSELVES and the truth is not in us. If we say we have not sinned we MAKE GOD A LIAR and His word is not in us'.*"

He sank back down in his chair and I never heard another peep out of him!

I anxiously waited for the next night and the verdict of those who had come from the solicitors' office. Mr Pinchbeck brought words of comfort to me. "Praise the Lord! They were very impressed. Two of them committed their life to Christ."

He then went on to say something that did my ego no good at all. "It was not the sermon."

The next bit of information showed me that God was at work: *"It was the way you dealt with that man who shouted*

114

out!"

That Portsmouth event still lives in my memory to this day. The only thing I can't remember is the date of those meetings!

It was in April 1955 that I felt we should hold a pioneer crusade in the town hall in Bridgwater, about forty miles from Bristol.

Bridgwater is, at first glance, like any other town, but it doesn't take long to realise that there is more to this industrial town than meets the eye, much more. Bridgwater's history starts almost at the beginning with an entry in the 1,000-year-old Domesday Book. Throughout the following centuries it has played an important part in the growth of the area. By 1402 it was a major shipping port in the west country and today it is a thriving industrial town, attracting many new businesses and major retail parks.

The team and I travelled back and forth each day to Bridgwater. We rented the Town Hall that seated between 400 and 500 people. It was hard. Some nights there were no more than thirty people in. However, we did start a church there. Now, sadly, it is closed. The self-accusing thoughts that came to my mind were not pleasant. "You messed that up! That was a big failure!"

I'm sure that it was God encouraging me when He showed me something that I had never seen before. We always judge evangelistic meetings by the number of people who commit their lives to Christ. For some people, however, to whom God has constantly spoken and who have just as constantly rejected His offer of forgiveness, God is graciously giving them one more chance. God has to use someone to give them that final chance. That person could very well be one who has subsequently been used by God to bring thousands to the place where they have committed their life to Christ. On another occasion, that same person becomes God's channel to give someone *their* last chance. God showed me that both these factors are part of evangelistic preaching.

God truly blessed us with a really outstanding prison ministry. Once every two months I was privileged to take about twenty members of the New Creation Singers with me for a Gospel service in Bristol Horfield Prison. The jail's chapel was usually packed. The tough prisoners seemed to look forward to it, but I have no illusions about why! There were two main attractions, one was a little extra time out of their cells and the other was the singing of the New Creation Singers. The prisoners probably thought that my 'little preach' was a price worth paying for the other two advantages.

We also held a two monthly Sunday morning service at Leyhill Open Prison, where the attendance was not quite as large. If you asked me now how we managed to get into both prisons on such a regular basis, I honestly couldn't tell you. During those prison visits I always tried to remember that God had promised that His Word will never return to Him void and there were certainly some inmates who came to faith in Christ. A great friend and colleague of mine, Rev Archie Biddle, was of great help and encouragement to them through a weekly Bible study he held in Horfield Prison. It always was a terrific rush to get back to the City Temple in time for the 11.00 am morning service but I have never once regretted the prison efforts.

CHAPTER 11

Telling the Good News

I have always been proud of my Welsh blood, and the 'Land of Song' was always dear to my heart. So I was very pleased that not long after Bridgwater I accepted an invitation from a personal friend to have a crusade in his church in Wales. Reverend and Mrs Alex Johnson had been leading the Elim Church in Holyhead in North Wales for a number of years. Holyhead was only a small town at the time and everybody seemed to know everybody else. Nowadays it is the largest town on the island of Anglesey and is perhaps known best for being a busy ferry port to Dublin. However, it is a bustling shopping and visitor area in its own right. The town centre offers an overnight stop on the way to, or from, holidaying in Ireland or as a centre for touring the island of Anglesey itself. We had little time to enjoy the wonderful scenery, walks and beaches.

Our Elim headquarters supported this evangelistic effort by paying the full rent of the hall which seated around 500. We began the first service at 8.00 pm on the Sunday evening. In a short time the opening night saw the town hall packed with over 500 people. In addition there were many who were unable to get in ... Many who came forward for prayer claimed that they were physically healed.

I remember that Tuesday evening when Howell and his

mother came to the service. Years earlier, he had been knocked down by an army lorry when he was just six years old. His mother told me, "We were in Liverpool last week and the medical specialist who usually sees Howell advised me that the best thing would be to have his arm amputated."

In the service that evening, I prayed for Howell in the mighty Name of Christ Jesus and told him to stretch out his paralysed arm. He immediately did so and an amazed crowd saw that God had healed him. The local press reported the event with:

'Revival' Heals Boy at Holyhead

We stayed for meetings in Holyhead Town Hall for two weeks. All too soon, the closing Sunday night of the crusade came. The service was timed for six o'clock. The Hall was full to capacity. They were still queuing outside. We began a second meeting at 7.30 pm and people were still queuing outside. We started the third meeting of the evening at 8.45 pm. As a team, we were virtually on the platform from six o'clock to ten o'clock. Yes, it was tiring! The press report summed it up as follows:

> "Remarkable scenes were witnessed recently during the crusade of revival and Divine healing. The opening night saw the large town hall packed to capacity with over 500 people. Great enthusiasm continued to the end of the crusade. Several of the older inhabitants said they had not witnessed any such scenes for over 20 years, whilst others were prepared to go back to the days of the great Welsh revival for their comparisons."

We had been privileged to see God move in such a mighty way. I don't know how many people came to faith in Jesus Christ that night but when we left Holyhead, the local

119

church was much stronger.

Come with me now to Ilkeston. This town is situated in the Erewash Valley in Derbyshire near the border of neighbouring Nottinghamshire. At the present time a large number of the people work in the textile industry, especially upholstery and lingerie manufacture. Although mostly an industrial area, it is surrounded by beautiful countryside.

Ilkeston's lovely Town Hall seated around the 500 mark. The opening night was an 8 o'clock service. It was a disaster. A congregation of 18 was scattered in every part of the building! I had the embarrassment of asking them to come to the two front rows! How different from Holyhead. *What is God doing to me?* I wondered.

But God did move in healing power, and the local paper carried reports of the many healings. They interviewed a number of them and photographed them. Still there was no great move in numbers attending. I tried everything I could to get that Town Hall even quarter full. I failed to do even that!

I remember going to our annual Elim church conference which was being held just one week after the crusade finished. I stood up and said, "Brethren, I'm sorry that the money that you kindly put into the evangelistic effort at Ilkeston has been wasted. There were only 118 conversions to Christ."

I'm glad to say in 2005 that the Elim Christian Centre in Ilkeston is alive and well! I was reminded yet again of the very simple truth that God had shown me some years previously. It is certainly worth repeating, so I am deliberately doing so. I personally cannot save one single soul. That is the responsibility of the Lord Jesus. I cannot even convict people of their sin. I might be able to make them feel uncomfortable, but that is not true conviction. That is the responsibility of the Holy Spirit. My responsibility is to TELL them! We must not fail the Lord or our generation. Church activity plans and even church building programmes fail unless they are used to enable us to better TELL out the message of His love and saving grace!

Weston-super-Mare is only about 14 miles from Bristol. It would most certainly be listed amongst the top ten seaside resorts in the country. It has a long beach which is pretty well packed in the summer months. There are hotels of all shapes and sizes from which to choose if you are looking for a seaside holiday.

Weston retains much of its original charm. There are still the lines of limestone houses, beautiful parks, piers and of course the sands. Nowadays, people often take several short holidays a year and the town has adapted to meet those needs.

The Town Hall in Weston is just about the same as any other town hall in the country. It has a central position in the town and seats about 350 people. In 1973 we booked it for a series of meetings. We were able to involve our Bristol City Temple musicians. We did, however, also invite a very gifted young man, Len Magee, to join us as our guest vocal soloist. Len had been with me on previous occasions. In addition to having an outstanding voice, Len also composed all his own songs. I feel sure that two of his most popular songs were 'The Presence of Your Spirit Lord' and 'He's Only a Prayer

121

Away'.

We were assured of good congregations because large groups of people from our church in the Bristol area came down every evening. There were also a good number of local people who attended. Many of them came to faith in Christ at that time and were keen for us to extend the series of meetings. To continue in the Town Hall was a non-starter. Would we be able to obtain the use of another hall?

I'm convinced that God moved. We were able to rent the local St John's Ambulance Brigade Hall that was well situated. It seated close to one hundred people. A young Irishman, Jimmy Ritchie, left college a little earlier than planned and became the first pastor of the new Elim church in Weston-super-Mare. We did, however, need our own building so that we could plan a full and active church programme. Then something quite remarkable happened.

Anyone travelling along the sea front at Weston-super-Mare can hardly miss seeing the spire of Holy Trinity Church. Holy Trinity also owned a super church hall just off the sea front. It seated between 120 and 150. It was just what we needed.

They sold it to us for just £8,500! It so happened that they needed the £8,500 to put a new heating system in Holy Trinity Church. The Elim pastor and people were very excited about the move to their own building. Brother Jimmy Ritchie remained as pastor of the church until October 1977. The church had prospered under his leadership but the "call of Ireland" was too much for him to withstand any longer.

Towards the end of 1977 Reverend and Mrs Robert

Griffiths moved to Weston and took over the Elim pastorate. God blessed their ministry in a very wonderful way. In 1983 two remarkable things happened. Firstly, Holy Trinity decided that they were going to sell their main church, and seemed quite keen for us to have it. Someone from the Bishop of Bath and Wells' office contacted Robert Griffiths and invited him over to Wells to ask if he was interested.

Robert's reply was just the one to be expected. "Yes, we are certainly interested but the big question is, how much?"

The next statement was quite amazing: "We would like to give it to you plus all the furniture and equipment"!

I think that in the end £1 changed hands and Elim simply had to pay the legal costs involved. They did make it clear that from the moment of possession Elim were responsible for the upkeep of the church. They did also warn of the Weston-super-Mare gales that would come from time to time.

I know this story might be hard to believe. There is no doubt in my mind that God was in it. Neither is there any doubt in my mind that the Holy Trinity authorities had been willing to listen to the directions of God as He was leading them. There can be no other explanation for the turn of events.

The second major factor was that the garage-man next door to our former Holy Trinity hall was keen to purchase it for the extension of his garage. I wonder why he had not tried to buy it at the time that Holy Trinity had sold it to us. He was now prepared to give us £30,000 for it. Since Holy Trinity had sold it to us for £8,500, I felt it only right to contact them and explain the situation. I would have understood if they had suggested that half the profit made on the sale should go to them. Yet they wanted nothing from the sale. They kindly said, "You use it for any work you have to do when you move into Holy Trinity."

There was something else that happened that was also remarkable. We were now moving into a church building which had a virtually new heating system that had been paid for with the £8,500 we had paid them for their church hall! We have still retained the name of the church as 'Holy Trinity'. Lots of alterations have been made on the inside of the church. The outside, however, still remains as it had always been. Robert and Joan Griffiths moved on in September 1984. They had experienced the blessing of God in quite a miraculous way during their time in Weston and I'm sure they will never forget it.

For a number of years Claude and Sue Ellerington have been the pastors at the Elim church at Holy Trinity, Weston-super-Mare. The church is flourishing under their leadership. From way back in the Town Hall days, God has certainly worked out His plan and purpose for Elim in Weston and His kingdom is still being extended.

Before leaving Weston-super-Mare I must let Mervyn Douglas tell you part of his story:

"The date of 23 July 1969 is indelibly imprinted on my mind. It was the day that I broke my leg as the result of a rash tackle in a so-called friendly soccer match. The game was immediately abandoned. I attended the Bristol Royal Infirmary and was able to see one of the leading orthopaedic surgeons, Mr Keith Lucas. He fitted a vanadium plate to the broken tibia in my left leg.

In order to assist in the research that was being done, I returned to the hospital for many months as various tests were carried out. I would be woken almost every night with the most excruciating pain in my right knee. I had the opportunity to mention the problem to Mr Lucas on my next visit to the hospital. After a thorough investigation of my knee, he informed me that I was suffering from osteoarthritis. I continued suffering for a number of months.

It was about this time that Pastor Ron Jones (of the City Temple in Bristol, a church that I had attended since boyhood) ran a series of evening services in the Town Hall in Weston-super-Mare. His assistant minister, Ray Craddock was with him. I was aware that my knee was painful and was very concerned about what the future would hold in terms of health, fitness and mobility. At the end of the service Pastor Jones announced that there would be prayer for the sick.

While many people were walking to the front, I was asking myself whether God could or would heal my knee. I was cynical about this kind of thing. There would have to be a molecular change in the bone structure. I could not imagine myself walking back free from pain, so obviously I could not believe that I would be healed. I then thought, 'Well, God must have healed someone as cynical and doubting as me in the past 2,000 years!' I really believed that. Waiting in the prayer line with many others to see Pastor Jones, I had further opportunity to contemplate.

Ron said, 'What's the matter Mervyn?'

I replied, 'I've got osteoarthritis in my right knee.'

Without further ado, Ron said, 'Let's pray!'

I can't remember much about the prayer, but whilst

125

Pastor Jones was praying, I became aware of the vastness of God, or as much as I could be aware of it. It was then that this awesome God spoke to me. He didn't say, 'I'm going to heal you.' He simply said 'Mervyn I love you!'

I walked back to my seat free of all pain with a slightly puzzled expression. What about my so-called cynicism now? I said to my brother, Richard, sitting beside me, 'I've been healed ... Doubting, cynical me.'

I thank God for healing my broken leg and for the expert help of the medical staff that ensured that the leg healed perfectly.

I thank God for healing my arthritic knee when no one else could help. Above all, I thank God for the most amazing truth that God loves me and wants me to love Him and to love everyone else that He loves too."

Mervyn Douglas is now pastoring a church in Clevedon with his wife, Joan. Clevedon is a town of some 23,000 people, on the coast of the Bristol Channel (Severn Estuary) in the west of England. Many large Victorian houses and public buildings survive today in the upper and seafront parts of town. Clevedon is nowadays a large dormitory town for the city of Bristol. The Clevedon Elim Church commenced with little more that ten people. There is now, in 2005, a membership of seventy people. I enjoy the privilege of being part of the ministry team.

When Mervyn was nineteen years of age, his Dad went to be with the Lord. Mr Douglas was a fully committed Christian with a truly anointed ministry. A service in the home was part of the thanksgiving to God for his life and witness. In the closing moments of the service, I simply posed the question, "Who is going to take this man of God's place?"

A young man came up to me within seconds of the close and said, "Pastor, with God's grace, I will do my utmost to take my Dad's place."

It was Mervyn, and he has certainly kept to that vow. God expects that kind of attitude and dedication from every one of us.

CHAPTER 12

Former Young Colleagues Reflect

I have already paid tribute to the fine young men who joined me in our witness in Bristol. Most of them came directly from college. Others came from very small churches where it had been mighty tough for them. All of them made their own special contribution to the ministry at the City Temple. Every one of them was 100% loyal. It is now a great joy to me to see how every one of them is being used by the Lord.

Rev David Holmes now reflects on those bygone times:

"The fields of the Lincolnshire fens glistened with the first snow of the winter of 1962. This lying snow contrasted with the heavy, dark skies that carried signs of yet more snow. It was a really bleak scene as the diesel train made for the destination of my first church after Bible College.

Inside I also felt a sense of bleakness and apprehension as to what the coming year held. The church that I was to pastor was only seven months old. It had come about as a result of an evangelistic crusade that had not gone well. I have since learned many times that the Christian life and ministry is a vocation and calling that is filled with God's surprises.

When I arrived at my destination, I went to collect my mail. The letter I received contained devastating news. It advised me that the Elim Executive Council had decided to close the church with immediate effect, before I had even arrived there! What followed in the letter took a few minutes to register. I was being appointed to Bristol City Temple as the assistant. As I held the letter in my hand, how grateful I was for God's wonderful timing. If that previous move had already taken place, I would have missed out on ever going to the Temple.

The man in the street often questions what a person or people in the public eye are like away from that gaze. For over twelve months of the time that I was at the Temple, I lived with the Jones family – Ron, Kath and their three girls. I had had the privilege of being brought up in a good Christian home. However, for me seeing the Jones family in the home environment was a Christian family par excellence.

In particular over the years since that time, I have marvelled how Kath maintained that quiet and gracious spirit for which she was known. She handled the needs and cares of her own family and ministered to others in a way that few in the Temple knew about. But – like everyone – even Kath had her moments!

Wednesday Night was designated for Bible Study. On one particular Wednesday evening we were running late. Someone in the family had delayed the usual leaving time. The trip into the city centre found Ron trying to get us there on time through the traffic. The nearer we were to the Temple, the faster he drove until approaching a road intersection it was too much for Kath. To the astonishment of all in the car, I am sure Ron in particular, Kath from the front passenger seat applied the handbrake to great effect!

I wanted to be a fly on the wall when they discussed her

action after church. Maybe they had a maxim – not in front of the assistant. There must be an insight here to the success of their marriage and ministry. Kath could put the brakes on Ron without him ever being hen-pecked!

Others in this book may pay tribute to Ron's evangelistic abilities, but for me his strengths lay in his pastoral heart. This can be said of Kath too. Ron officiated at child dedications, marriages and funerals, with such sensitivity. I have rarely seen this human touch bettered over years. Watching him minister at these events has had a lasting impact and influence on my own ministry.

I appreciated being given difficult situations to handle that took me on steep learning curves. For example, the first funeral that I took on my own was of a little boy about two years of age who had died of an accidental fatal overdose. His parents had come from overseas and were starting a new life in the United Kingdom. The child had reached out from his highchair into a sideboard drawer and had taken the tablets from there. My pastoral experience like this at the Temple filled a vacuum that no Bible College curriculum could do. In this I am very grateful to the Lord.

Few who have served as an assistant pastor somewhere, will not feel that sometime they have drawn the short straw. One of mine was Ron's request that I visit every 2 - 3 weeks an older lady, an adherent of the Temple, who sadly had a phantom pregnancy. This went on for over 12 months and as a single guy at the time, I confess my pastoral ability in the matter soon dried up! To this day I have no idea if Ron passed on the difficult ones like this to the assistant on occasions ... Oh, I'm sure he didn't! Or did he?

There was a fitting conclusion to my time at the Temple. Ron brought all these things together when he officiated at Dolores' and my wedding. We then moved to another pastorate but took with us happy memories of friendships with both the Jones family and Temple members which have lasted over 40 years."

After Bristol, David and Dolores Holmes took a large portion of the responsibility of the small church that we had opened in Keynsham. They always showed a real concern for people and their needs. They moved on to pastor their own larger churches, and God's rich hand of blessing continued to rest upon them as it does to this day.

Rev David Woodfield came to Bristol directly from college. David's favourite way of bringing any service alive was just to ask the congregation, "Are you glad you came?"

I'm glad to report that – ninety-nine times out of a hundred – I'm absolutely sure they were glad they came! I never dared to try it. I knew it would not have worked for me! David now holds an executive position in the Elim movement. As he recounts now, he has his own memories and his own way of telling his story:

"I turned up at the home of Ron and Kath Jones on the bank holiday Saturday afternoon of 1964. After surviving two years of uniformed National Service and two years of Bible College training I arrived right in the middle of the Bristol City Temple's August convention. There was no time for a settling-in period. I was thrown right into the proverbial deep end of this busy, thriving church and do not remember

ever getting out of it!

The word 'mentoring' was not in vogue in those days, but that is exactly what happened to me. I was mentored for two quality years by a man who had great communication skills and great sensitivity to the moving of the Holy Spirit. Ron Jones was a man who was truly a 'people person'. He expected us to work as hard as he did, and I reckon sometimes we actually beat him!

I will never forget the first time that I preached at a Sunday night service. Ron was away on his travels overseas and there was no visiting preacher, just me! The church was full. It was a nerve-wracking experience. All went well until near the end of my message. There was a loud interruption. Something I had said really upset a man in the congregation. I simply could not get him to quiet down. In the end, four of our strong deacons picked him up and carried him out on their shoulders whilst he was still shouting at me all the way down the aisle. I can still hear him!

I recall, too, a prayer meeting night when I was on my own. Quite often there would be spiritual gifts exercised, such as a message in tongues or a prophecy, in our prayer meetings. Frankly, I had never been used to interpreting a message in tongues. I spent a lot of that day praying that there would be nothing like that on that particular evening. God completely ignored my prayer and it all seemed to happen that evening! All I can remember is standing up, taking a step of faith and saying, 'This is what the Lord wants to say to you.'

A whole prophetic word followed. That experience opened up a new avenue of ministry for me in the use of spiritual gifts.

Ron Jones loved his cricket and I remember the Saturday afternoon that he was visiting a hospital to see someone who was quite ill. I was quite impressed. It was not until the Monday that he informed me that the schoolmasters cricket club was playing a game in those very same hospital grounds that very same afternoon. Hitting two birds with one stone, Ron had accomplished both engagements. It was most helpful for me to know that he was truly human after all!

I had met a Swiss young lady in College and it was whilst we were in Bristol that Pia and I were married and set up our first home in the ministry. Many of the deep friendships formed in those early days in that city remain to this day.

They were great days for me at the Bristol City Temple. I have an abiding memory of that dear church. It was full of life and vitality with great children's and youth programmes. Conversions and healings took place on a regular basis. Divine worship was vibrant and relevant. In a nutshell, for most people, myself included, it was said to be 'the best Sunday night in town'. Being at Bristol made a lasting impact on my life that – praise God – has served me well over the years."

Now it is the turn of Rev Stephen Hilliard to recall his memories associated with the Bristol City Temple:
"As the London train pulled into Temple Meads railway station in Bristol one Saturday afternoon in July 1969, I was conscious that a new phase of my life was about to begin. Bible college training was behind me and my first pastoral appointment lay ahead. Was I nervous? Of course I was, but

I was also excited. At last, God's call was taking shape in my life. I was about to become assistant pastor in one of Elim's largest churches, working under the direction of a man who was already a household name in our Movement and who in years to come, would fill the most senior offices – as President and General Superintendent.

The first thing that I remember about Bristol was the warmth of welcome that I received from so many in the City Temple. Pastor and Mrs Jones's kindness and encouragement were outstanding. I was never made to feel that I was just another assistant passing through. I do not recall Pastor Jones referring to me publicly as 'his assistant' (though that is what I was). He always called me 'my colleague' or 'my associate'. I was given opportunities to preach and my mistakes were graciously overlooked or tactfully corrected.

The first time I ever heard him preach was on the Sunday evening following my Saturday arrival. Earlier in that same week, the Rolling Stones pop group had caused outrage. They allegedly made blasphemous remarks about Jesus at one of their concerts. Ron Jones seized the opportunity to make his Gospel message relevant. It was entitled 'The Message of the Rolling Stones for this Generation'.

With tongue-in-cheek, his text was 'What mean ye by these Stones?' (Joshua 4: 6). Though certain liberties may have been taken with the text, the message was dynamic and challenging. Ron was always an outstanding preacher. He never engaged in controversy for its own sake. His purpose was always to challenge, encourage, teach and help.

I quickly discovered that the City Temple was a church ahead of its time in many ways, not least in its music, which was of the highest quality. Even drums were played during the services – a novelty in the mid-sixties! The drummer was excellent. The congregational singing was vibrant and thrilling. Powerful preaching and dynamic worship do not always go hand in hand, but they did in the City Temple in those days.

Although the church was large, it had an intimate family feel about it. There was none of the sense of loneliness that sometimes accompanies large numbers. In the Temple, individuals did matter. From the first, I was impressed by Pastor Jones's ability to pinpoint those who had been missing on the Sunday. To me, the congregation seemed a sea of faces. But to him, it was made up of individuals whose presence was appreciated and whose absence was noted. I not only watched him in action in the pulpit, I saw him sitting in the homes of the elderly, praying with the sick, comforting the dying and providing practical care where this was needed. I have known no one who could better comfort the bereaved at a funeral and, at the same time, present the Gospel in uncompromising power.

On each of the Christmas days that I was in Bristol, the pastor and his family would forgo the usual 'Family get-together'. They, along with others in the Temple, provided a Christmas dinner and an afternoon of fellowship for many who would otherwise have been on their own.

Ron Jones was a strong leader. He was the boss and I knew it and so did the congregation. But discipline was always exercised with grace and patience.

I do not think I could have had a better start to my ministry than I had there. I quickly learned that only the best

135

is good enough for the Lord and His work. No task is too menial and no person too insignificant for a good pastor's attention. I learned that God's work is not built on controversy but care, and that attention to detail is vital. I am grateful to the Lord for those days at the City Temple. They certainly made an impact on me then, and on my on-going ministry."

1970 was a very important year for Kath and me. We had been to South Africa for special meetings a number of times at the invitation of the Full Gospel Church of God. The executive council of that movement had invited us to take over the leadership of one of their churches in Cape Town. The possibilities were good and such a project had a measure of excitement. Cape Town is one of the loveliest places in South Africa with its magnificent Table Mountain and outstanding scenery. We, of course, had to take into consideration the future of our three young daughters but most important of all the question we had to ask was, "Is it in God's plan for us?" God had to show us, but how?

It was the Elim Churches' annual conference in May 1970. Leaders of the movement in South Africa had come especially to the conference to discuss any possible final arrangements. We chatted on the Sunday. It seemed good but Kath and I still felt the restraining hand of God upon us. It was vital that He made His plan very clear. The Monday came. One of the items for discussion was the appointment of the President-Elect of the movement. Whoever was voted into such a position would serve as the President of the movement from May 1971 to May 1972. A number of names were nominated. Out of that number I was chosen.

I confess that there were others on that list, I believe, who deserved the honour much more than I did. Kath and I could only conclude that God had used that appointment to show us that a church in Cape Town was not in His diary for us.

In the third and final year of Stephen's stay with us I was touring the churches at home and abroad. I had no worries or concerns about the church in any way while I was away; it was always in good hands. Stephen eventually left us to take up the pastorate of his own church in the Bournemouth area. In 2005 God continues to bless the ministry of Stephen and Jennifer Hilliard as they serve the Lord in Northern Ireland.

I would now like to take you back to 4th May 1970. It was the evening of my induction as President of the Elim movement at their annual conference. Kath was by my side and our three daughters had requested to have a spot in the service. They had evidently worked hard and secretly on a poem for the special occasion:

FATHER, DEAR FATHER

Solomon had wisdom when he wrote his proverbs down
And we're certain that you'll prove them by and by.
But there's one faithful saying you may have overlooked –
An omission we would like to rectify.

In Proverbs two and twenty and verse six or thereabouts
There's a saying and the words of it are these:
"Train up a father in the way he ought to go
And when he is old, he will not displease.

So we listened to its wisdom and commencing there and then
We embarked upon a programme straight away
To study up the Scriptures, no stone to leave unturned,
We started out to train him day by day.

The first command we studied was Ephesians six and four:
"Provoke not your children unto wrath"
And whene'er we "did the dishes" we suggested he might try
To prove himself "a true man of the cloth".

Alas it never worked, so we tried another tack;
We persuaded him to polish his car-old
And the verse we used to help him was Acts thirteen, forty-six
Where it states that Paul and Barnabas "waxed bold".

Again it was a failure so we had one final fling,
When garden weeds at home began to shoot;
Not wishing to be rude, we read a verse in Jude
That evil should be "plucked up by the root".

But we've utterly failed, as him we have assailed,
And today we here present our father Ron:
He may have failed the test, but our Dad he is the Best.
Dad we love you
Eluned
Glen and Non.

CHAPTER 13

First Attempts

The first attempt we make at almost anything can be fraught with problems. That certainly was the case with my first attempt at radio broadcasting. It came about in quite an unexpected way.

It was at the end of a Sunday morning service in the City Temple in 1962 that a smartly dressed man wanted to speak to me. He had been advised to come and chat with me by someone from the Christian Herald newspaper. He wanted to write a something of my story. We made arrangements for him to come to our home and simply have a general chat. As a result, Ron McCatty wrote a booklet about me that he felt might be of interest to some people. It was no big deal really. However, a copy of the booklet reached the offices of BBC Radio in Bristol.

The BBC must have found something in it of interest. They invited me to visit the studio. An outstanding broadcaster, Frank Topping, was the director of religious broadcasting. We chatted for a little while. Amongst other things, he wanted me to tell him why I chose to enter the ministry. At the end of our time together he said, "You have a good voice for broadcasting. Would you like to do five three-minute 'Thoughts for the Day'?"

I was thrilled. I couldn't wait to get home to tell Kath the exciting news. I phoned her. He wanted just a few 3-minute talks. I thought that this was going to be one of the simplest things to carry through. It was child's play ... Well, that's what I thought!

Events proved me to be completely wrong. It did take me a little longer than I expected to complete the scripts. I read them through with a feeling of satisfaction and a sense of pride ... *Wow, Ron Jones on air!* I phoned Frank Topping to let him know that I was ready for my first broadcasting session. It would not take long to record five 3-minute broadcasts. Forty-five minutes at the most.

Frank Topping read the first script and lifted a blue pencil from his desk. I had the sinking feeling that this broadcasting business was not going to be so easy after all. When he had finished it was almost impossible to read any of my 'brilliant' scripts for his blue pencil lines. Why on earth had I bothered? The whole thing was humiliating. It became even more humiliating when he began his observations. "You're not supposed to be conducting an evangelistic crusade, you know."

Of course, I knew it was not possible to conduct a crusade in three minutes flat. But it was the way he said it that troubled me. He had not finished with me or my effort yet. "It's very unlikely that you will even be sowing any seed either."

I had honestly thought that was the whole idea. He then reminded me that before I came on, the listeners would be listening to a programme of all types and styles of music and that when I finished they would return to the same kind of music. I was to be an intrusion into their breakfast-time listening. I was 'the God Spot' and although they would not turn off their radio, they would turn off their minds until I got off air. Then they could continue on listening to what they really wanted to hear. If that truly was the case, why bother at all? Then came Frank's pearl of wisdom. "It's important to remember that, in most cases, you're just turning over the soil."

I saw it immediately. It is a Bible principle. There must be the turning over of the soil before there can be the sowing of the seed. That is very much the case in our ungodly generation. I saw very clearly that day that I must seize every opportunity to just 'turn over the soil'.

I was greatly impressed that day with Frank Topping's patience with me. We did complete the five broadcast recordings but it did take two and a half hours! The beauty of it was that they still sounded like mine ... only different! Following that first attempt, it was 'in-and-out of the studio' in no more than forty minutes which included a cup of coffee! Eventually, Frank never even bothered to read the scripts in advance.

One of my highlights in those early days of radio broadcasting was in the Holy Land. I must have told Frank that Kath and I were going there.

He simply said, "Good, you can do some programmes out there. I'll give you one of our best portable recorders and it will be no problem to you. Just do five 5-minute recordings at different locations and we'll use them when you get back."

He made it all sound so easy, and that worried me. We were there from the Palm Sunday right throughout Holy Week. The preparation to do what Frank called "a few simple programmes" was quite an experience in itself. Kath was the guinea pig. I recorded her reading my scripts over and over again, trying to make sure the correct buttons were pressed and that the volume was at the correct level. It all became a bit of a nightmare. Frank Topping had always done this sort of thing and had bags of experience. I was still only very much a learner. Somehow, we managed.

I was quite proud of our Palm Sunday programme in Israel. I was able to start it with the braying of a donkey. I had to follow that donkey for many hundreds of yards and then be sure that I pressed the 'on' button just at the right time. I am not sure how many attempts I had but, at long last, there was the sound of sweet success. It brayed yet again, but this time I had it on tape! Our Palm Sunday programme began and ended with a braying donkey!

We managed the other programmes quite well too. One was by the Sea of Galilee with its lovely rippling waters and serenity. Another was in the Garden of Gethsemane which vividly brought back to our minds the awful agony of Jesus in that garden. We could almost hear the sound of marching soldiers and the heart-breaking desertion of His disciples. It was a moving experience.

Of course, the final programme was in the Garden Tomb, the place where the cold corpse of Jesus had been placed. It was guarded by Roman soldiers on watch just in case something remarkable happened! It was the pathetic scene of what appeared to be the end of a decent man.

But that day, both Kath and I caught something of the atmosphere of the Resurrection Day. It was terrific. I will never forget it – JESUS IS ALIVE!

He is my contemporary Saviour and Companion in life

and He has promised to be with me to the very last inch of my earthly journey! What a promise! And He is certainly keeping it!

That day in Jerusalem brought back memories of my dear daughter Glen when she was just four years of age. She was playing at the bottom of our stairway with her friend Vivienne from over the road. As they sat there, young Glen started to do her preaching bit: "Jesus was a good man! He healed people! He was very kind to everybody! But cruel men deaded Him!"

I must admit I had never heard the word 'deaded' before. After about thirty seconds, she loudly continued her little homily: *"BUT HE DIDN'T STAY DEADED!"* The grammar was pretty hopeless but the truth was mighty powerful!

Perhaps the most moving Holy Land programme was the one we did in the dirty Jerusalem dungeon where Christ Jesus probably spent His last night before going to the Cross. My script went something like this:

"Sitting where I am just now, I cannot help but recall what must have been the greatest miscarriage of justice of all time. I am right here in the Palace remains of Caiaphas the High Priest. I am actually in the dungeon where Jesus might well have spent His last night before going to the Cross. Caiaphas was the person who set in progress this so-called 'Trial of Jesus'. Let's face it, if any trial was rigged – it was this one!

"There were so many people who managed to get their finger in the pie. Ah yes, there was the cruel Roman Governor Pilate. There was the sly foxy King Herod, there was Traitor Judas and the religious leaders who were

determined to see Jesus die.

"The Bible records, 'and Pilate gave Jesus to them (the crowd) to be crucified'. So they made Jesus pick up the cross as they shouted out the most dreaded of all things: 'Hey you, take up your cross!'

"This meant just one thing ... He was to die. A cross was only used for dying on! I feel as I sit here today at the very spot where this awful crime was perpetrated that I would like to conduct my own inquiry into the case. Let's interview some of the folk who were heavily involved in the trial.

" 'Calling Pilate's wife!

" 'What do you think about Jesus?'

"A deep breath follows and then she speaks: 'Have you not heard that I sent a very urgent note to my husband the Governor pleading with him not to have anything to do with condemning that just man?'

" 'How about you, King Herod? You mocked and had your bit of fun taking the mickey out of the Lord Jesus?'

'It's strange that you have asked me that question. Have you not read that I sent Christ back to Pilate and told him in no uncertain terms that I found no fault in him?'

" 'Calling Judas Iscariot!

'It was you who sold Jesus out for thirty measly pieces of silver. You must have come to the conclusion that He was a deceiver or you would never have done anything like that. What guilt did you find in Him that made you feel compelled to hand Him over into the hands of the authorities?'

"Tears come into the eyes of Judas as he replies, 'Don't mock me! When it was all over I could not find peace because of my own guilt. I took back that blood money and made it clear to the authorities that I had betrayed innocent blood, but they just would not take any notice!'

"And what about the judge himself?

'Roman Governor Pilate, you were the judge in this case. What do you now think about the verdict?'

'Well, history will record that I knew for sure that He was not guilty. I said so publicly and plainly. I even went to the trouble of taking water and washing my hands in front of the people in order to make sure that they knew that – for my part – I was certain he was not guilty!'

"As a result of all we have heard from these witnesses, I am bound to ask myself, 'If everyone concerned in the trial declared Christ to be innocent, why then did He have to die?' I look into my own heart and see my greed, selfishness and sin. They make me feel guilty. Yes, that's exactly it. Jesus took my place and your place and that's why He had to die!"

When we returned home to the UK, Frank Topping was really impressed with the Holy Land radio programmes. So much so, after using the recordings on successive mornings on BBC Radio Bristol, the nationally networked BBC Radio 2 broadcast them. They linked them together with some excellent music and a quality reader of scripture with an outstanding voice. The programme was entitled 'Journey of a Lifetime' and broadcast mid morning on the following Good Friday. Within the next six months, Frank moved to London. He was promoted to the position of Director of Religious Broadcasting for BBC Radio 2.

Blessing the airwaves!

Some time later, my living room telephone rang. It was Frank. After a quick hello, he asked, "Will you do some 'Pause for Thought' scripts for the Terry Wogan morning radio shows?"

I consented and the BBC gave me my own introductory signature tune entitled 'The Rhythm of Life'. I have to admit that I hated it! If you ever get hold of a copy of the tune, you will understand why!

The talented ace DJ host, Terry Wogan, always introduced me as if he and I had been friends for years. I have always felt somewhat embarrassed by that. People say to me, "What kind of person is Terry Wogan really?" I have to confess to them that Terry Wogan and I were certainly not bosom pals. Indeed, I have to admit that I never ever set eyes on him in person! Such is the wonder of broadcasting.

I have always enjoyed broadcasting but I feel sure that I would never have made it had it not been for the help, advice and patience of Frank Topping. Another brilliant radio broadcaster/producer who has helped me and encouraged me throughout the years is Trevor Fry who presently (in 2005) has his own programmes on BBC Radio Bristol.

After a few years of broadcasting, the BBC invited me, with seven other ministers from various denominations, to Broadcasting House in London. At the first session the BBC Head of Religious Broadcasting gave us an excellent talk on the secrets of good broadcasting. It was then across the road, over to nearby All Souls Church. We each had to preach a twelve-minute sermon.

It was a self-conscious time for us all and the vacant atmosphere was not at all helpful. Preaching to seven other preachers plus the BBC Head of Religious Broadcasting was certainly not all that exciting. To be honest, it was most frightening. We wondered what would happen when we arrived back at Broadcasting House and the evaluation session started.

I did not come out of it all that well. Most of them felt that I had been too evangelistic and said so in no uncertain terms. I was glad of the Roman Catholic priest who was in the group. He gave me full support. The BBC provided excellent hotel accommodation. The next day, the schedule was similar. We again received a talk from the BBC Head of Religious Broadcasting on compiling five-minute 'Pause for Thought' scripts. I was so glad that Frank Topping had already schooled me in this type of broadcasting. The second day was certainly a better day for me than the first! Looking back, I am very thankful to God for the many broadcasting opportunities that I have been given to declare the truth of His Wonderful Love.

Now let me tell you of my very first experience of preaching through an interpreter. It must have been in the mid-fifties or sixties, I think. A group of my minister friends and I travelled by road to the World Pentecostal Conference in Sweden.

Our first stop was Belgium. Arrangements were made for us to have some food and sleep at a local Pentecostal Church. Part of the arrangement was that between those two events (eating and sleeping) we planned a service for the church. I was chosen to be the preacher. As this was my first time of preaching through an interpreter, I planned to preach a sermon with which I was fairly familiar.

The pastor's wife was my interpreter. She was brilliant. She gave me great confidence. I had hardly finished a sentence when she followed me. It was an excellent meeting and I felt that I had taken the whole thing in my stride. This preaching through an interpreter was not all that difficult after all. However, there was a fine well-educated young man in the congregation who was on home territory. The church in which I was preaching that evening in Belgium was his home church. Yet I knew him because he had visited our church in Bristol. Naturally, I made a point of speaking to him afterwards. After the usual polite beginnings to such a conversation, I mentioned what a brilliant interpreter the pastor's wife was.

His reply was something of a shock: "Brother Jones, we have had two sermons tonight. The one that you preached and the one our Pastor's wife preached. I believe, Brother Jones, that our Pastor's wife told the congregation tonight some home truths that I'm sure she has been wanting to tell them for a long time!"

I did say that it happened forty or fifty years ago. I reckon that I know that it couldn't possibly happen nowadays. Too many people overseas know and speak English as well as we do. But that was my first experience. Probably, on that occasion her sermon bore more fruit than mine. I certainly hope so!

CHAPTER 14

Headquarters Calling

Twenty-five years had passed since Kath and I followed Reverend P. S. Brewster's pioneer crusade in the Bristol Colston Hall. Nearly thirty years had passed since we followed him to the new Elim church in Caerphilly.

He was now in 1977 retiring as General Superintendent of our Elim movement. A special executive council meeting was called to pray and discuss who his successor should be. We met in a Bournemouth hotel. Eventually the council voted by secret ballot on the issue. To my utter amazement they nominated me. I phoned Kath to tell her. It was something we had not expected. We did, however, accept the vote of my contemporaries as being God's direction for us.

I made one condition: that the secret ballot at the ensuing conference accepted the nomination with an overwhelming majority. This happened. Kath, our youngest daughter Eluned and I moved into a super house at the foot of Leckhampton hill, in the lovely town of Cheltenham, and on the first day of May 1977, I took up my task as General Superintendent of the Elim Pentecostal Churches. Pat Tillett (now Mrs Pat Ellis) was my very efficient and helpful secretary and I'm pretty sure she got me out of many a hot spot.

It was certainly different, sitting behind an office desk for almost the first time in close on forty years. I was now trying to help in making plans for a movement instead of a large lively city church. I had to care about a dedicated office staff instead of dedicated and sometimes needy church members. Some of the church members were new converts. Some of them had been with me since the early days of the City Temple. In the new job, I hardly ever conducted a Sunday morning communion service. This was something that I greatly missed.

Every weekend, Kath and I would be away preaching in one of our Elim churches. People were extremely kind to us wherever we went. They usually made our visit a 'big church event'. In reality it was our privilege to meet so many of our Elim pastors and their wives. It was a joy to be able to encourage them in their work for the Lord Jesus and to sometimes give a little helpful advice regarding a problem or two. However, for Kath and me, it was somewhat strange. We missed the joy of seeing new converts growing in the Lord. Probably it was because I was a pastor at heart and Kath was a true pastor's wife at heart.

During those years we were holding our Elim Annual Conference mainly at Clacton-on-Sea where one will find at least seven miles of clean sandy beach. The conference attendance would always be around 5,000 people. In the course of four years I was able to arrange with the BBC for us to have two 'Morning Worship' services at conference. We also had one Sunday evening 'Sunday Half-hour' hymn singing broadcast on BBC Radio Two. The BBC Director of Religious Broadcasting gave me the privilege of introducing

151

the hymns on that occasion. I was nervous but excited. I suppose, to some large degree, these broadcasts came about because of those two days spent at Broadcasting House in central London.

One memorable Sunday evening we had an IRA terrorist bomb-scare. It was thought that it might be a warning from the outlawed Irish Republican Army. It could not have happened at a more inconvenient time. I was leading the meeting. Reverend Denis Phillips was preaching. He was going well. Then the urgent alarm warning came. We did manage to get about 2,000 people out of the hall in quite an orderly mode as we awaited the police and fire brigade. Apparently it was a bogus scare, for no bomb was found. Eventually we were able to return to the hall now encased in a tense atmosphere. Nevertheless, Denis continued his sermon quite brilliantly!

Business sessions could be difficult. I recall one occasion when I was chairing the conference. Things were going quite well. We were well ahead of the time schedule. Some members of the conference attributed that to the fact that when we did hit a difficult spot in the business I got them to sing a suitable chorus and have a word of prayer! It did work most times!

The one occasion when it definitely did not work centred on where a comma came in a proposal. I cannot even remember what the proposal was, but that comma still haunts me! The discussion went on for a couple of hours. At last I just had to use my 'guillotine powers' to curtail the matter of dispute. I think I lost a few friends in the process!

Always an innovator, Kath commenced a conference

afternoon time of fellowship for ministers' wives and sent a monthly letter of encouragement to each one of them. Widows of ministers too were not forgotten. The letters and phone calls of appreciation that Kath received made it all worthwhile.

It was quite late one Monday evening in 1978 that I collapsed with severe chest pains. Urgently, Kath sent for the doctor. She arrived very quickly, and diagnosed a bad heart attack. At about midnight, the ambulance arrived and took me to the Cheltenham Hospital. All the usual tests were carried out immediately. Kath was told that the following twenty-four hours would be critical. I am glad to report that I survived them. The staff in Cheltenham Hospital were terrific. At the end of two and a half weeks' hospitalisation, I was back home. However, one of our doctors took Kath aside and seriously remarked, "You have to know, Mrs Jones, that your husband is living on borrowed time."

Worse was to follow. Soon I was back in hospital. The situation was not good. My friends from the Elim Office, Tom Walker and John Smyth would come up to our home to keep me in touch with the latest news from the churches around the country.

One dreaded day, my own GP, Doctor Benney, called. Kath sat by my side on the bed. He sat at the foot of the bed. Eventually he told me: "Mr Jones, I'm sorry to tell you that you must face the fact that you will never preach again!"

Kath and I were shattered. It was our life! Quite suddenly the bottom had fallen out of our life. That night was a very restless one for us both! Then the very next morning something remarkable happened.

It came in the form of a letter from Guyana in South America. I had visited our churches in that country a few times. Sister Tempow had founded an Elim church in part of her house in Middle Road, La Penitence. She was one of the most remarkable Christian ladies that I have ever met. A great preacher with a strong personality, Sister Tempow was an expert at training young men for the work of the ministry. They would then go out and plant new local churches in other parts of Guyana.

Sister Tempow was the writer of the letter that arrived on our doormat that desperate Tuesday morning. We had always exchanged Christmas cards since I first visited her church. This, however, was the very first time she had written to me. She was never one to waste words. She wasted none in this letter:

"Dear Brother Jones,
I have been thinking about you a great deal over the past few days and I believe that God has given me a special Scripture for you.
Please read ISAIAH 41, 9-10. God bless you."

I did not have to look it up. It was the very scripture the Lord had given me at two o'clock in the early hours of a Monday morning forty years previously. It was the same scripture that caused me in my early twenties to go to see the secretary at the local gasworks later that Monday and give in my notice. Please forgive me for putting it in print once again. It has always been so inspiring to me in my Christian life and ministry:

'You are my servant, I have called you. I have chosen you and have not cast you away; fear not, for I am with you; be not dismayed, for I am your God. I will strengthen you. Yes, I will uphold you with my righteous right hand.'

WOW!! Here was God's own message straight to Kath and me via Guyana. And the end was not yet! The following day I received a letter with a Blackpool postmark. It was from one of Elim's younger ministers. It was as brief as was Sister Tempow's letter, and it read:

> "Dear Pastor Jones,
> You have been an encouragement to me many times.
> I just want to encourage you.
> The scripture I feel I should pass on to you is ISAIAH 41: 9-10."

Today, writing this book in 2005, it was 27 years ago that my Doctor Benney told me that I had to face the fact that I would never preach again. Since that day I have preached thousands of times! There are moments when I wonder why God still leaves me here. He must still have some purpose and plan for me.

It was on Friday 23rd June 1978 that we received the horrendous news that nine of our Elim missionaries and four of their children had been murdered in Rhodesia (now Zimbabwe) by 21 terrorist-guerrillas. They had come over the border from Mozambique and cruelly attacked the missionaries with axes and other weapons. It was one of the blackest days in Elim's history. The sheer brutality of the Vumba massacre shocked the world and was front-page news. It happened during the period that I was virtually house-bound as a consequence of my heart attack.

All the missionaries at the time of the tragedy were talented, highly qualified and committed to the task of not only proclaiming the Good News of the Gospel, but also giving practical help and encouragement to all in need. Three of them had science degrees.

Peter McCann and Philip Evans were teachers with B.Sc. Degrees.

Roy Lynn was a whiz with mechanics and Joyce (his wife) was a nurse/midwife.

Wendy White had a degree in social studies as well as being a nurse.

Catherine Picken was a sports teacher.

Mary Fisher (teacher) had a B.Sc. Degree.

Irishman Robert Lynn, who was familiar with the troubles in his own country, had access to a gun. This was mainly used for shooting snakes and vermin. However, he, together with the others, agreed that they should be completely committed to neutrality in the battle for power in Rhodesia. It was a battle between the forces of the Rhodesian Government under the leadership of Prime Minister Ian Smith and those of the so-called 'liberation forces' led by Joshua Nkomo and Robert Mugabe (now President of Zimbabwe).

The missionaries' first impression of the Vumba (where this terrible tragedy took place) was that it looked similar to the English Lake District, so beautiful was the mountainous area. It soon changed to a place of martyrdom.

This was one of the saddest and most frustrating times in my life. To hold the position of General Superintendent of the Elim Pentecostal Churches and not to be able to do much to help at such a time was well-nigh soul-destroying. I did, however, have the opportunity of giving a few interviews to the press and TV. Kath and I kept in touch with members of the families at home by letter and phone. We sought to encourage them in the tragic loss of their loved ones. I still cherish the expressions of thanks from many of them for the little we were able to do at that time. It seemed to mean so much to them.

When earlier I was writing about the City Temple's yearly youth-camp at Llanmadoc in South Wales, I mentioned the name of Mary Fisher. I told of the Friday night around the campfire at the top of a small Welsh mountain when she threw a twig on the fire. You will recall that when I asked her why she had done so, she said that she had just told the Lord that she was prepared to go wherever He wanted her to go. Mary was one of the nine missionaries who were murdered. Every one of them will certainly have received a great reward in Heaven. Each will also have personally heard those comforting words from the Master. *"Well done, good and faithful servant!"*

On Sunday June 25th 1978 special services were held in Elim churches all over the United Kingdom. Some of the press reporters who went to those services were astonished when they heard many ministers and members praying for the very people who had committed the murders. The Daily Mail on 26th June carried the headline:

'FATHER ... FORGIVE THEM!'

Elim's long-serving Missions Director, Reverend Leslie Wigglesworth who had then just retired, was invited with his successor, Reverend David Ayling, to the British Foreign Office. There they met with the then Labour Foreign Secretary, Dr David Owen. Some time later, when David Owen was giving a TV interview regarding his personal faith, he paid tribute to those two ministers. They had asked if they could pray with the Foreign Secretary, and they were given permission to do so. In his TV interview, David Owen said that they had greatly impressed him. He added that it was probably the first time ever that such a thing had happened in that office!

On the very day that the tragedy took place, Reverend Peter Griffiths (Principal of the Elim School in Rhodesia), was the guest speaker at the Elim Bible College Open Day in Surrey. He and his wife Brenda were home on furlough. In January of 1979, Brother Peter Griffiths and Brenda returned to what was by then Zimbabwe. Amazingly, he was given a senior position in the Education Department of the newly independent Zimbabwe!

As a result of the attitude of forgiveness and prayer, I and many others believe that Elim's missionary work in Zimbabwe has flourished rather than diminished. The secondary school is now twice the size it was before the massacre. The hospital is making excellent progress. The church is growing and sixteen new churches were opened between 1993 and 2003. It has also been reported that some of the 21 terrorist-guerrillas have come to faith in Christ since that dreadful event.

There is now a plaque that holds a place of honour at the Elim Church Headquarters in Cheltenham. It reads:

IN GRATITUDE TO GOD
FOR THE LIVES AND SERVICE
OF OUR MISSIONARIES MARTYRED
IN THE VUMBA, RHODESIA,
23 JUNE, 1978.
Peter and Sandra McCann, Philip and Joy; – Wendy White
Philip and Sue Evans and Rebecca; – Catherine Picken
Roy and Joyce Lynn and Pamela Grace; – Mary Fisher
"THEY LOVED NOT THEIR LIVES UNTO DEATH."
Revelation **12: 11**
WE MUST NEVER FORGET THEM.

My first preaching engagement following my heart attack was some months after the massacre of our missionaries. It was at a European Pentecostal conference in Holland, where I was to preach through an interpreter. There were almost 2,000 people present. Kath was understandably very anxious.

She told me afterwards how the Lord had spoken to her just before I began to preach. "God reminded me of Psalm 46, verse 10: 'Be still and know that I am God'."

The truth of that verse became so real to her that she wrote about it in one of the contributions to the daily Bible reading book Vision for Today. It has been an encouragement to me ever since, and because I feel it might be a blessing to readers, I present it here:

BE STILL AND KNOW

BIBLE READING: PSALM 46.

Verse 10 almost seems to be out of place, like a piece of a jigsaw puzzle that simply does not fit. The Psalmist speaks of shaking mountains, raging nations, tottering kingdoms, desolation and wars. Then in the midst of all the chaos and confusion comes this verse, "Be still and know that I am God". One day, on reading this psalm I began to realise afresh that in the midst of all these seeming calamities God was in control. Furthermore I discovered that the literal meaning of "Be still" is "Let go". The Psalmist is really advising us to "Let go and let God" ... "Let go and know God". If I believe that God is in control of the whole universe then why should I be holding on so tightly to the reins of my life? The Psalmist is telling me that if only I will "Let go" I will prove God. This is exactly what Job did. His family and his possessions had gone, his wife and his friends failed him and his own health was in tatters, but listen to these words: "The Lord gave and the Lord has taken away, blessed be the name of the Lord" (Job 1: 21). He then goes even further: "Though He slay me, yet will I trust Him" (Job 13: 15). Job had certainly let go of earthly things and proved God in a most amazing way. "Lord, please give us faith like that."

THE ABOVE WRITING WAS THE LAST ONE KATH COMPLETED BEFORE ENTERING INTO THE PRESENCE OF THE LORD.

I resigned from the office of General Superintendent on May 1st 1981. I just trust and pray that Kath and I were able to contribute something of spiritual help and leadership to the Elim churches in the United Kingdom and, even more importantly, that we were able to contribute something of lasting value to the Kingdom of God. I can only leave that with the Master.

At the very same conference I was nominated and voted in as Elim's President-Elect. I began my second term as Elim President on May 1st 1982. It was our joy, yet again, to be able to visit many churches in this country and overseas. This time it was without the heavy responsibility of being General Superintendent.

CHAPTER 15

Return to Bristol

When I first left the Bristol City Temple for the Elim Headquarters, my good friend Pastor Archie Biddle and his wife were inducted as the new ministers of the church. Archie was a minister of long experience who had pastored large churches. The Bristol church continued to experience the blessings of God. Unfortunately, Archie's retirement day came all too soon and once again, it was all change.

In the meantime, with Kath by my side, we were enjoying my second term as Elim's President. It was during this period that I had the joy of doing something I had long wanted to do. The Elim Church in my home town of Swansea was a flourishing one. The minister and his wife, Reverend and Mrs Lionel Curry, received an urgent call to the mission-field to work in Ghana. The Swansea Church was going to be without a pastor for three months. I simply couldn't help but grasp the opportunity of fulfilling a lifetime's dream! Kath and I volunteered to go and fill the gap. Those were three great months.

Our home was still in Bristol but the officers of the Elim Church furnished a manse so that we could stay in Swansea whenever we wished. God graciously blessed our ministry there and we would have loved to stay; but age had crept up on me and I had already retired twice!

It was on a cold, wind-chilled 17th of November 1982 when the phone rang at our home. The news was not good. It was one of the City Temple officers who explained that the membership there was going to be split. It is always sad when this takes place in any church. It adversely affects young people, older people, families and relationships as a whole. The current minister at that time was leaving with close on half of the City Temple congregation. They were going to start a church in another part of the city. The news was devastating to us. Then came the request: "Will you and Mrs Jones come back and consider helping us?"

Initially, I have to admit that I was not at all keen on the idea. What would it be like, returning to a church that would be about half the size it was when we left it? People would most certainly feel very downhearted. Kath was adamant. "No, Ron, I definitely do not feel that we should go back to Bristol!"

Later in November, Kath and I were at the Elim Church in Coventry. I was preaching there as part of my 'presidential tour'. It was a good service. Afterwards, we got into our car and followed the pastor to his home for lunch. We had only gone a few yards when Kath said, "Ron, God has spoken to me in the service this morning. It was during the time of the 'breaking of bread' (Holy Communion) part of the service that God told me we should go to Bristol. I'm willing to start there on Monday!"

Without further ado, I phoned our headquarters first thing on the Monday morning and told them that we were willing to return to the City Temple Church in Bristol. The officers and members were delighted. We recommenced our ministry there on 23rd January 1983 and remained there until 15th August 1988.

It was tough settling back into the pastoral work at Bristol. The discouraged people were now coming to a half-full congregation and some of their family and friends had gone. I did my utmost to lift their spirits and my own. The first six months were the hardest that Kath and I had ever experienced in our ministry. She was a tremendous support to me yet again and God certainly strengthened us both. If He had not, I don't quite know how we would have coped and come through it.

Just about six months after our return, the legendary American evangelist Dr Billy Graham held one of his large Mission England meetings at the Bristol City Football Stadium (Ashton Gate). Wonderfully, God certainly blessed the event. Thousands of people attended the meetings and many of them committed their lives to Christ.

Around the same time, BBC TV was broadcasting nationally a movie called 'The Day After'. Well written and directed, it was very moving and somewhat frightening in the light of the Cold War that was the dangerous status quo between the West and the Soviet Bloc. The film sought to portray what the situation on Earth would be like for ordinary people after a nuclear war. Many in society were genuinely frightened and were looking for answers and solace

Then an idea came to me – but I can't say for sure that it was God who brought it to my mind. But I like to think that it was!

I said to myself, "What about starting a series of similar

meetings in the City Temple, the day after Billy Graham finishes at Ashton Gate?"

The idea turned into a positive plan; but who could I get to conduct it? Then the name 'Don Summers' sprang to mind. He had conducted large evangelistic crusades in every part of the United Kingdom as well as overseas, particularly in America and Mexico. Don was also an associate evangelist of the Billy Graham team and he lived just around the corner from us.

Thankfully, Don was free to come for five days beginning on the next Sunday, the very day after Dr Graham was due to finish his Mission. With the BBC movie and Billy Graham's Mission in mind, we simply called our crusade: 'The Day After'.

By God's grace, we never looked back. That first Sunday drew a surprisingly large number of new people who came along to the event. The New Creation Singers sang better than they had ever sung before. Don Summers faithfully preached the Gospel under the anointing of the Holy Spirit and during the five days of meetings, forty or so people came to faith in Christ Jesus.

Amongst the newcomers were Wally and Diane Marriott. After the Sunday evening service, Wally came up to me and said, "Reverend Jones, in a few weeks' time on a Saturday evening, I'm planning a Royal Air Force event in Yate. Would it be possible to hire the New Creation Singers choir?"

Wally didn't need to hire the Choir. The singers were all there, pleased to oblige, grateful to God for the opportunity of presenting the Gospel message at such an event..

I will never forget the marvellous group of people we had.

They somehow managed to get along to just about every meeting that we held. We were beginning to see and feel a real revival-spirit again. There was no doubt in our minds that God had brought us back to Bristol.

It was not much more than two years later that my hips became quite troublesome and painful. Indeed, I had to walk with the aid of two sticks. We had to leave our house and go into a bungalow because I couldn't manage stairs.

I was now 72 years of age and had told the church officers that I would have to finish at the end of the year. It was during that period that I was booked to preach at the World Pentecostal Conference in Zurich, Switzerland.

Kath and I made our way to central Europe and, reaching Switzerland, settled into the hotel already booked for us. With my handicap, I found it was most difficult trying to get around.

Saturday night came. The stadium was superb. The congregational praise and worship was soul-stirring. Then it was my time to preach. I struggled onto the platform and preached with the help of an excellent interpreter. The subject that I was given was *'Jesus, the only hope for the world's future'*. There were about five thousand people from all parts of the world present. The service ended. I was tired and just wanted to get to the taxi that would take Kath and me back to the comfortable hotel.

I was on my way out of the stadium when two men (who I had never seen before) stopped me. If you asked me now for their description, I couldn't give it to you – apart from the fact that they were of medium height and not very smartly dressed. To be honest, I was not happy; I just wanted to get back to the hotel and my bed. Looking me in the eye, one of the gentlemen spoke gently: "We have a word from God for you."

At that point, I was even less happy. The alarm bells started ringing. I thought to myself, "God knows my situation. If He really does have a message for me, surely He could give it to me directly."

I just had to listen further to the gentleman because I did not wish to appear rude or even unspiritual. The man then said, "Pastor Jones, God wants you to know that you will reach more people with the Gospel in the coming days than you have reached in all your previous years in the ministry."

I thought, "How crazy can one get? I'm 72 years of age and on two sticks. I'm going home to tell the people of my church that I will have to finish at the end of the year. This guy certainly has a terrific imagination or else he lives in a little fantasy world of his own."

Back at the hotel, I told Kath about the event. She made no comment but I had the feeling that she thought exactly as I did. I went to bed and put that foolish message out of my mind. "If God has a message for me He has to speak to me direct. That's final as far as I'm concerned!"

But He never did seem to speak to me directly!

Some members of the City Temple had come to Zurich in order to encourage me at the Conference, and we all stayed on in beautiful Switzerland for a week. Our accommodation was close to a very lovely lake. One day, my friend Colin Packer hired a small boat for two. He got into the boat and kindly helped me in, sticks and all! Kath said, "Ron, you shouldn't be doing that, it's crazy!!"

She was right, yet again. Colin's daughter decided she would like to come along with us too. She sat in the middle. I did feel a little anxious but dared not show it. We were quite a way out when young Debbie decided to stand to her feet. Then it happened. The boat shook and then capsized!

Within seconds, a man, his daughter and his pastor were in the lake, all fully dressed. We had to swim for it. The problem was that I can't swim a stroke! Naturally, I went under water at once, while Colin was struggling to get the boat the right way up. I'm fairly sure that I was going under for the second time when thankfully, he did succeed. I managed to get a grip on some part of the boat and Colin reached out and dragged me in.

Not knowing whether to laugh or cry, I was just like the proverbial drowned rat. Kath and our friends who had come with us stood on the lakeside frantically shouting for help. No one offered any real assistance. People were gawking and probably concluded that it was just a group of crazy folk messing about. Little did they know how completely wrong they were! Kath and our friends were genuinely afraid that I would have a heart attack. Yet, here I am in 2005 and as you can appreciate, I survived and am still around to tell the story.

Since then I have thought about the Apostle Paul's Malta shipwreck experience recorded in Acts chapter 27. That sounds like quite an exciting adventure that would make a great Hollywood movie. Instead of 'three in the boat' there were '276 of them in the ship'. The timber ship went aground in the surging waves and the violent gale smashed it to pieces. 276 people ended up in the raging foam. Some of them were grateful that they had taken swimming lessons when they were young, as they were most probably first ashore. But what about those poor doomed ones who couldn't swim? The 'no hope' sign was up for them. I love how the Bible records it: *"And the rest, some on boards and some just grasping hold of broken pieces of the ship ... they all escaped safely to land."*

I have imagined a few of them telling their amazing story to their grandchildren years later. I can almost see the wide-eyed kids sitting transfixed on the edge of their seats:

"Do you know children, it was the most terrible storm I've ever seen. There was rain, waves, gales, thunder, lightning ... I felt sure I was going down for the third time when a piece of the broken ship happened to come along. It came just at the right time! I grabbed it! I was one of the last ones to reach shore. But I made it, thanks to that piece of the ship coming my way when it did. D'you know children, I feel sure God sent it, don't you?"

Well, that's how I would have told it anyway! I'm pretty sure that many times afterwards the children would say, "Granddad, please tell us that shipwreck story again."

On many occasions since I have thought of that incident, I just wish it had come to mind that day on the lake in Switzerland. I have found it quite thrilling in my life to see how God sends His little planks along just at the right time. Just sit down quietly for a few moments and think back over the years. I'm sure that you too will remember a few of those God-sent planks!

The waiting time for hip replacement surgery was 18

months and that's assuming that they could find some brave surgeon who would be willing to tackle me in view of my bad heart condition. Whilst Kath and I were away in Switzerland, the members of the City Temple took up a special offering so that I could have the operation performed privately.

My doctor soon found an excellent surgeon who was willing to carry out the operation. He did, however, warn us that there was an extra risk in my case.

With the New Year celebrations over, on 3rd January of the following year, I was in hospital, and the operation was successfully performed. Soon I was back preaching in the City Temple on the last Sunday in April without a walking stick in sight.

In 1987 I was invited to visit the Vision Channel TV studios in Swindon. Some friends who were already involved in the work of the Channel kindly took me to the studio. There I met Fran Wildish for the first time. Fran is quite a remarkable woman of vision and perseverance.

Some years ago when the government encouraged towns and cities to try to establish their own local TV stations, Fran saw it as a challenge to Christians. She started with a half-hour children's programme. It must have been considered successful because the Vision Channel was the first Christian channel in Britain to receive a government licence for showing Christian programmes on cable TV.

After the polite hellos, we had coffee and cakes across the desk. Then Fran asked our friends, Ken and Ruth, to be seated on the settee. She then turned to me and said, "Ron, will you do a seven-minute interview with them? I need something like this for publicity purposes."

I was shaken. 'For publicity purposes' might well have been true but I very soon had the feeling that I was on trial. It was part of a process of checking out whether I would be any good for TV interview work. Ken and Ruth had already told her of my radio broadcasting experience.

I must have passed her test. Fran said, "Ron, will you do some TV interviews for us? I'll make sure that you have a first-class cameraman and we'll soon arrange for a good sound engineer too."

She was certainly right about the cameraman. Phil White is a committed Christian (with a terrific sense of humour), and a brilliant cameraman, and a quality film director. We have since become great friends. Better still, I had the thrilling privilege of baptising his daughter Debbie.

I was anxious to have my own choice of sound engineer, but who would it be? God had one right on the spot. He specialises in things like that! The very first wedding that I conducted in Bristol over 50 years ago was that of Roy and Grace Waterman, and it was Roy who soon became our sound engineer at the City Temple. He was thrilled to be part of our Vision Channel TV team. Since then, we have filmed over eighty programmes together, in the series called 'On the Road with Ron Jones'.

We have met some interesting people in the process, including: popular singers Helen Shapiro and George Hamilton IV; trucking business entrepreneur Eddie Stobart and his wife Norah; Captain Brian Walpole OBE (one time head of the Concorde Division of BOAC); the well-known BBC tennis commentator, Gerald Williams; and the outstanding international evangelist from Germany, Reinhard

Bonnke.

Helen Shapiro's story of her giving up smoking is one programme that I shall never forget. She admitted that she was smoking around sixty cigarettes a day. After her acceptance of Jesus into her life she told me that she made a promise to the Lord in March that she would give up smoking around November time. Helen then told me of the day in that very same month of March, when she was going into a newsagents for some cigarettes and there in the window was the notice that read 'Remember Today Is No Smoking Day'. She decided there and then that God had brought the date forward!

Most of the people I have known who have given up smoking have said, "Pastor, I've thrown all my cigarettes in the rubbish bin. I've finished smoking and this time it's for good!"

But not Helen. She told me that she went home and smoked most of the cigarettes she had in the house. Her husband John went for a long walk as he had witnessed Helen's previous attempts to give up smoking and he simply couldn't stand seeing any further attempt. She then went to bed and in her own words she said, "When morning came I felt all clean inside."

From experience, I know the same kind of feeling.

George Hamilton IV is a hugely successful Nashville country & western singer and yet is one of the most humble men that it has been my privilege to meet. When I asked him how he would like to be seen as a role model, his reply was clear, direct and swift. "Ron, I don't want to be remembered just as someone who has sung on the 'Grand

Ole Opry' show in the USA or at the Palladium in London. I'd prefer to be known as a man who walked his talk! And you know Ron, some of us Christians don't make a very good job of that!"

Sadly, he was right.

My television interview with the former BBC tennis correspondent (known for his Wimbledon commentaries) was a most moving experience. Gerald Williams told me of the time when he was at the top of his career yet at the same time his personal life was just about in tatters. He told me that he had a Bible at home but seldom read it. Indeed, he said that he gave very little thought to God. Emotionally, he declared, "Ron, my life was in such a mess that I took my Bible to my bedroom and just cried out loudly to God, 'PLEASE HELP ME!' "

Gently, before the camera, I asked, "Did He help you, Gerald?"

Gerald's response to my question was quick and brief: "He certainly did!"

As we came to the close of the interview, in his own way, he told me of an incident in his life when God made a tremendous impact on him. *"It was the final night at the Seoul Olympics in Korea. I was at the Olympics as the BBC tennis correspondent. The final race, a marathon, had been run and I was returning to my hotel. I found it difficult to understand why people were still lining the street. I wondered if the President might be coming that way.*

"I arrived at my hotel and just waited to see what was really happening. There was the sound of light handclapping

that became louder by the minute. A man came into sight. He was just staggering along. He looked as though it would be impossible for him to take another step. Surely, he was not a marathon runner. That had finished more than half an hour previously. Almost immediately behind him a white ambulance came into sight. They were following him just to pick him up when he collapsed. It seemed like that would take place at any moment.

"On he came. He was the last runner in the Olympics. He had already passed three underground stations and could very easily have pulled out of the race. I watched him passing and as he did, God spoke to me and challenged me. He said, 'This is for you and you know where it is in the Bible ... You don't have to be some successful preacher ... You don't have to be some great hero for me ... You have started the race and all I ask is that you finish the race ... When the cameras are not whirling and there is no limelight and no one sees you, will you make sure that you finish the race?' " (See Hebrews 12:1-2.)

I do want to finish the race to His glory and I hope that you – the reader – do too.

I recall asking the great TV preacher from Germany, Reinhard Bonnke, about his very first crusade. I know that he can now draw many thousands of people to his meetings. He said, "Ron, my first crusade was held in a mud hut and the congregation numbered five!"

He was only three better than me!

I am told that in 2005, at the time of writing, the 'On The

Road' TV programme goes potentially into approximately seven million homes every week on the Vision Channel on Sky digital TV.

Having listed these rather fascinating recollections, I now take you back to the Zurich conference and remind you of the two gentlemen whose 'message from God' for me, I had concluded to be rubbish. One of two men had said, *"Pastor Jones, God wants you to know that you will reach more people with the Gospel in the coming days than you have reached in all your previous years in the ministry."*

To be truthful, I had completely ignored their message simply because I didn't believe it! Many years later, suddenly, God's word came back to me in the contemporary context of seven million homes every week plus many more homes in parts of Europe. Sure enough, my TV congregation must total many more people than I have previously reached in all my years of ministry.

Those men were right after all! I had completely overlooked the fact that our God specialises in things thought impossible! Yes, I must admit that (like the disciple of old) I still have to pray the following little prayer from time to time: *"Lord, please help Thou my unbelief."*

CHAPTER 16

I Believe

Over the years I have been asked what lessons I have learned in the area of leadership. Perhaps the most important one is how truly amazing it is that God uses such frail people as us. To talk about leadership in an exclusive kind of manner is something that I find quite difficult in case readers shut off and feel this part is not for them. I am therefore glad of the incident related in Acts chapter 8 which tells us that *'They who were scattered abroad went everywhere preaching the Gospel.'* They were not the 'big shots' of the early Church, but the fire of God burned in their hearts and their lips caught fire too! I have a feeling they might well have become leaders of small groups of Christians in homes or even underground. Back then, there was not a seminar or teaching tape in sight!

My mind goes back 3,500 years and I imagine a possible Jewish ghetto in Pharaoh's Egypt. There we witness the worst sort of cruel slavery that it is possible to see. The taskmaster is there with his whip and the poor slaves are speedily being forced back to their task even though they can hardly stand.

Then we leave the ghetto and make the journey to a farm in another country. There is just one Hebrew man at work in the wild fields there. He has been there daily for just about forty years minding some sheep. He seems to have a good business going. Well, not really – those sheep are not even his own. They belong to his father-in-law.

It is a usual working day except for "that bush". He had never seen anything like this before. It has caught fire but there are no ashes. From that bush, great flames are leaping upwards and a Voice is heard. That must certainly be no less than the Voice of God. *"Moses, I want you to know that I have seen the oppression of my people in Egypt and I have heard their cry because of their taskmasters, and I know their sorrow. So I have come down to deliver them out of the hand of the Egyptians and to bring them into another land."* (Exodus 3:7-8.)

Moses must have thought, "What a tremendous relief, God Himself is going to do something about the situation at last!"

He had probably been praying for something like this to happen for forty years and now God was actually coming down to deliver them! I'm not quite sure whether this good news got back to the ghetto. If it did, there must have been great rejoicing. God was on His way!

Then it was all an anticlimax at "the bush". The Voice said to Moses, *"I know the people's plight, Moses ... I have seen their suffering, Moses, and I have heard them ... I am coming down to deliver ... Come now Moses, I'm sending YOU!"* ((Exodus 3: 10.)

That must certainly be a Divine mistake! There was disappointment for Moses and those in the ghetto. It was not God who was coming after all. It was only Moses and who wanted Moses anyway? The Divine Task was much too big for him and, in any case, he had made a complete mess of things forty years ago. The Hebrews had to accept the fact

177

that it was only Moses coming when they expected God. How amazing, God's answer to the situation was Moses. Likewise, so it must be that God's answer to our world situation is you and me. Don't ask me why. I just felt God telling me that He wanted me to be part of His answer to the world's needs. I marvelled at it. I was humbled by it. It is not just for men and women at the top. It is for all who truly believe. Today the Lord is saying, *"Come now, I am sending you!"*

Now comes one of the most vital questions in the whole scenario. *What really are the important truths and factors I must embrace in my life if I sincerely wish to be used by God?*

Number one for me is that I must seek to serve the Lord in the area that is God's calling for my life. We sometimes put square pegs in round holes, but God never does! Christ in Matthew chapter 25 gives us the graphic picture of the distributed talents and their uses, reminding us that it is "to each according to his several ability". As Christian believers, God has a task for each one of us and as surely as we seek Him, we will find it.

That very fact raises a challenging question: Why do I really want to be used by God anyway? Is it a deep desire to serve the Master or is it a little bit of investment in power or even a spot of self-glory? How can my motive be tested? I believe that one day the Lord showed me the answer. I cannot remember whether I was reading the incident which took place between Christ Jesus and Peter the disciple after the Resurrection, or whether it just crossed my mind.

Jesus asked, *"Peter, do you love me?"*

The disciple's answer was swift. *"Yes Lord, of course I love you!"*

The Master replied, *"In that case Peter, go and feed my lambs!"*

A similar question came from Christ a second and third time. *"Peter, do you love me?"*

Peter's answers and Christ's commands were similar. *"Yes Lord, for certain I love you!"*

"Go and feed my lambs and my sheep."

Then it hit me! Jesus did not say *"Peter, do you love feeding lambs and sheep?"*

That was not the important question. It was: *"Peter, do you LOVE ME?"*

We must love Him more than the task we do for Him, no matter how big and important or however small and insignificant!

For anyone anywhere who is seeking to serve the Lord there is often the destructive power of discouragement. Through the years, there have been times when I have been discouraged. At times, I thought I had a brilliant idea which turned out to be a complete flop. The devil uses this discouragement as a weapon in a most masterly way. God showed me that I was not the first of His children to feel discouraged and that I would certainly not be the last.

I read of a man whose cry was rather pathetic. He actually wrote his feelings down and they went something like this: "I have laboured in vain!" That was bad enough, but there was worse to follow. "And I have used up all my strength for nothing!"

Thank God I have never reached that stage. Who was this poor discouraged man? He was the very man to whom God entrusted the truth of the Incarnation, the truth of the Cross, and the truth of the Gospel message. The very same man who was able to say, *"God called me from my birth and made my speech like a sharp sword."*

Yes, it was Isaiah the prophet! What had happened to make such a man feel such a failure? It was discouragement. He had invited them to come and they had ignored his invitation. The Living Bible puts it like this: *"I have spent my strength for them without response."*

Thank God that he did get it sorted out and wrote, *"But for certain, my just reward is with the Lord and my recompense is with Him."*

I was greatly encouraged when reading through the letters written to the early churches in the first few chapters of the Revelation. I already knew that every letter carried a different message to each church because each one had differing needs and circumstances. What I had not noticed previously was that there was just the one phrase repeated and in every letter the Lord says to each one, *"I KNOW YOUR WORKS."* *The Righteous Judge of all the earth knows what I do, and sees my motives if no one else ever notices. That very fact should be our daily encouragement. The Apostle Paul had certainly grasped this truth when he wrote in 1 Corinthians 15:58. "Therefore, my beloved brethren be steadfast, immovable, always abounding in the work of the Lord, knowing that YOUR LABOUR IS NOT IN VAIN IN THE LORD".*

I love David's response to the incident where he and his victorious army were returning to Ziglag, and when the city came into sight the flames were leaping upwards. There was a scene of destruction everywhere. An enemy army had come and abused their wives and children. Their property was ravaged or gone. The triumphant singing of a victorious army turned to weeping. The strong army men *"wept until they could weep no more"*. A scapegoat must be found. The cry went up: *"It's all David's fault."*

They picked up stones to stone him. That certainly was rough justice. What about the discouragement factor for David? It was there, but he had a foolproof remedy. *"And David ENCOURAGED HIMSELF IN THE LORD."*

Thank God, whether we hold some important position in church life or we are just quietly seeking to follow the Lord where He has placed us, we can do the same! We can sit and just remember the "goodness and mercy" that has followed us thus far in our lives.

I believe that early in my ministry I began to realise that – if I was going to be used by the Lord in a meaningful way – it was vital that I had a love and concern for people. I knew that such concern would make certain demands upon me. I admit that I have not always met them by any means.

For instance, it would call for patience with some people who rather annoyed me and even, sometimes, discouraged me. I had to be willing to accept that there might well be an unknown reason for their action.

It would mean that I would sometimes have to give time to listen to people when I don't particularly want to listen to their problems, their grievances with others, and – quite frequently – their suggestions and advice for me. I soon found that it was sheer folly to expect perfection. I saw very clearly that leaders are people with flaws who are marvellously called by God to help, encourage and lead other people with flaws!

I very quickly learned how very much people needed encouragement simply because I quickly found out how much I needed it myself. This is a 'Barnabas ministry'. Acts 11:22-24 does not tell me that Barnabas was a great preacher or an outstanding Bible teacher or even a good Gospel singer. It just tells me that he was a good man, full of the Holy Spirit and faith. It also tells me that when he came to the church at Antioch and had seen the grace of God (I'm sure, as in most churches, there were other not so good things to see) he was glad. He then *"ENCOURAGED them all that with purpose of heart they should continue to follow the Lord."*

After all my years in the ministry I still need motivating. So do most other Christians. Not simply commitment to loyalty but a <u>commitment to excitement and enthusiasm</u>. A commitment that makes people feel that "this is too good a thing to miss out on"! I am always inspired whenever I read about Nehemiah. He was only a King's cupbearer in a foreign land. Yet he heard about the conditions of Jerusalem's broken walls and burned gates. If one had gone on a tourist trip to Jerusalem at that time, the guide might well have said, "Those walls and gates have not always been like this, you know. If you had come here a few years back, you would have seen stately walls and splendid gates. But, sad to say, that is no longer the case!"

Everyone had probably thought it was sad, but not one of

them had done anything about it. That is, not until Nehemiah came along and everything speedily changed. One inspired man with a vision from God so inspired the people that they cried out, *"Arise, let us build!"*

Nobody had thought about that before. Of course, Sanballat and all his discouragers came alongside the builders saying, "Come down! Pack it in! If a fox leans against that wall it will collapse!"

The response was swift from one builder: "Not likely, we are doing a great job and we will not come down!"

Of course, there are pitfalls that await all of us in our desire to be useful in God's service. Being too busy to pray is certainly one of them. Falling victim to the snare of pride is another. Yet another is getting discouraged by cynical criticism. Probably one of the most serious pitfalls is neglect of our own family.

Way back in those war years of 1942, I believe God impressed on me a very important truth regarding my usefulness to Him. It came when I was at my second church (South Kirkby). I was listening to an outstanding Bible teacher, Donald Gee. After so many years, I cannot remember very much about his sermon. But I still remember its thrust. He spoke about the incident in the book of Acts where seven deacons were appointed by the early Church. Donald Gee then went on to declare that in most churches he knew, where deacons had been appointed, the number was seven, whether there were seven who merited or not! "This," he declared, "was imitation and not obedience!" That hit me. I must never mistake imitation for obedience.

A number of years ago a great friend of mine built a very large church on the principle of 'door-to-door evangelism'. It seemed a simple plan. Church members knocked on doors, spoke to the residents, left some literature and a personal invitation to the church. It worked. A best-selling book was written about it. A number of churches and church leaders felt it was a good plan. I was amongst them. The problem was that it did *not* seem to work in most cases!

The vital truth is that I have to hear from God what is His plan and purpose for me and not just feel that all I have to do is imitate His plan and purpose for someone else. The proverbial 'church-around-the-corner' may have a terrific band and worship group, brimming with musical talent. However, I must never let the devil make me believe that because our church does not have such a band, consequently our usefulness to God is curtailed. I have tried to always remember that God's word to me is simple and clear: *"Obey Me and never be content with simply imitating what seems to be going on around you!"*

Serving God is the highest calling and we are in this together. The story of the miraculous catch of fish in the Gospel of Luke chapter 5 is not only exciting, it is illuminating. When they couldn't cope with the huge catch they called to their partners in the other boat. This is the only place where the word PARTNERS appears in the Bible.

It is gloriously true that we are many members with diverse gifts, talents and abilities in the Master's service. Therefore, we should be 'not lacking in diligence' but 'fervent in spirit, serving the Lord'.

CHAPTER 17

You'd Never Believe It

It happened on an eventful Saturday evening in 1980. Kath and I had been invited to Rock Church, a well established church and a widely known church in New York City's heart, Manhattan. Pastor Vic had been the pastor of Rock Church for many years. This time we could easily detect that he was a sick man and was looking much frailer than on our previous visit.

Rock Church, over its many years, followed the same pattern. They invited guest speakers for two or three weeks at a time. Kath and I used to arrive by taxi at around lunchtime on the Monday. The super little lady, Sister Gertrude, was quite an amazing lady. She was both the official caretaker and the treasurer. After enduring our seemingly endless traffic adventure, she was always awaiting us at the door with cash in hand ready to pay our taxi driver.

I must admit that I disliked the next part of our arrival sequence. It was struggling with the suitcases up at least fifty rather steep stairs to the visiting preacher's apartment. It was by no means lavish. The furniture was pretty old. The TV had to be tapped fairly hard in order to get any sound out of it, let alone a picture!

All visiting preachers from the United Kingdom had to pay their own airfare to America. Some of my friends, who had been to the Rock Church to conduct services, advised me that it would be difficult to cover the airfare for two, as they only gave a ministry gift of $300 a week. In advance, we worked out our budget carefully and felt that we could just about break even. It was not ideal but it was worth the experience and the opportunity.

On the first Sunday evening, Sister Gertrude came to our apartment and handed me an envelope and just said, "Pastor Vic told me to give you this."

When we opened the envelope there was a cheque for $1,000. We concluded that we had been given our gift for the three meetings early on in our visit. That was not so. Each Sunday evening Sister Gertrude came along with an envelope with the same little statement: "Pastor Vic told me to give you this." Each time it was $1,000.

We were kept very busy. The first meeting was on the Tuesday afternoon followed by another meeting the same evening. Then there were the meetings on Wednesday, Thursday and Friday evening. Saturday was the day off! Sunday was the big day. Sunday morning at 10.30 am, Sunday afternoon at 3.00 pm and the evening at 6.30 pm. Pastor Vic always preached on the Sunday afternoon and that was the best-attended service of the week no matter who the visiting preacher was.

Rock Church was in one of the busy avenues off an even busier avenue that I think from memory was called Lexington Avenue. On our first free Saturday evening, we decided to do a little more exploring of Lexington Avenue, with its large stylish departmental stores and its many fast-serve hamburger joints. The Avenue was crowded with fast-walking pedestrians. We had only gone a few hundred yards when a voice cried from over my shoulder, "Hello! Fancy seeing you here!"

Neither of us could remember seeing this smartly dressed, well-spoken dark-skinned young gentleman previously. But since he knew us, we stopped and chatted. We told him we were at Rock Church just around the corner from where we were standing. He kindly warned us never to go on the New York underground railway system. He said that he was mugged twice in the few months he had been there. As we chatted, he seemed to know Bristol pretty well. He certainly knew the City Temple too and had actually attended there a few times with his father when he had lived in Bristol. I tried to work out who in the church back home could be his father. At that time, we only had a few gentlemen in the church with ethnic backgrounds. I mentioned that fact to him.

I said, "One of the people from an ethnic background is among the most faithful members that we have and he's one of my church officers. That's Renford Daniels."

It seemed to come as no surprise to him. I understood why when he said, "I know, Renford is my Dad!"

I was just a little surprised that Renford had not mentioned it to me. However, I was glad to know that Renford was anxious to support his son as much as he could when the lad was in quite a reputable college in Manhattan. It was nice to meet up with a young man who might have felt a little bit homesick and just have a chat with him about his home city of Bristol.

In those early minutes I did most of the talking. Renford's

son was certainly a good listener. However, he did say, "When I told my Dad about the two muggings, he was quite concerned and sent me some money to help me buy a small car."

We chatted about his car and the difficulties of driving in a large American city. He said, "I came in my car today and did some shopping. I parked my car in Fifth Avenue and when I came back someone had siphoned out all the petrol. A passing gentleman saw my plight and directed me to the nearest petrol station. I went along and hoped that they would loan me a petrol can but they wanted $5 for it and I just didn't have $5. I hadn't brought much money with me today. Would you be able to loan me $5, Ron? I'll come along to the service at Rock Church in the morning to make sure you have your 5 dollars back."

We loaned him the $5. We just had to, if it was only for Renford's sake. He accepted it thankfully and we continued walking and chatting. I thought our chat was coming to an end but then he told us of another problem. "The $5 will only be sufficient for the loan of the can. I'll need another $20 for the petrol."

I thought to myself, "Of course he does. I should have thought of that earlier. An empty petrol can is of no use to a car that has no petrol in it to start with!"

We were being conned in the most gentlemanly way. I refused. Our chat ended and he was on his way with our $5. My friend Renford was certainly not his father and he had certainly never been inside the Bristol City Temple! We never told Renford of that particular incident. The next morning, however, I did tell the folk in Rock Church. There didn't seem to be any sign of an ounce of sympathy. As a matter of fact, they seemed to think it a big joke. I felt they might be thinking, "Our guest preacher for these couple of weeks can't be very bright to be caught out with an old trick like that!"

A lovely little coloured lady came up to me after the church service with a few words of comfort. "Brother Jones, I was thinking about you at 6 o'clock this morning and the Lord told me to give you $10."

When we arrived back in our apartment, Kath and I wondered what might have happened if we had given him the other $20!

Freda attended our church in Bristol very occasionally ('Freda' was not her real name). One fresh bright morning at breakfast time, the phone rang at home. It was Freda's sister-in-law to let us know that Freda was seriously ill with cancer and that she would like us to visit her. The sister-in-law explained to us that Freda was on her own most of the day because the rest of the family were out at work. She said that if we gave her an approximate time for our visit, she would make sure that the key was left somewhere outside the front door so we could get to see Freda.

Kath and I went along the same morning. We picked up the key and let ourselves in. Freda certainly looked seriously ill. The doctor had inserted a number of tubes. We stayed with her a little while, prayed with her and left. Every morning, the faithful sister-in-law would ring up to let us know how the night had gone and to enquire whether we would be visiting during the day. She wanted to make sure that the key was left in the same place. Every day was the same. Our visiting was daily. Quite often, we would call to see her after an evening service. The doctor would always leave some medicinal tablet to give her before we left her for the night.

The young pastor who was with me in the church at that time was Pastor John Bradley. John had spent some time in a medical college where those who were preparing to go to the overseas mission field would receive some training. John was staying in our home and some days he and I would visit Freda together. I still recall times when John was so moved by what he had seen that he would leave the meal table with tears in his eyes and go to his bedroom to pray for her. One day when Kath and I visited her, she was actually spitting up blood and looked desperately ill.

It was the national public holiday, 'August Bank Holiday weekend' and we were holding a series of special meetings at the church. Freda's sister-in-law phoned the church, "Can someone please come and pray with Freda?"

It was certainly helpful that there was a registered nurse in that service. She offered to go and see Freda. The family were away for the Bank Holiday weekend. When the nurse returned from visiting Freda, she called me aside and said, "I don't think that lady will survive this week."

We all prayed and Freda survived the week and lots of future weeks. The sister-in-law faithfully continued to phone every morning.

Christmas came and went. It was now Easter time and I was in a London church for some special meetings. Kath phoned me. Freda's mum had passed away and the funeral was to be on the Easter Tuesday. Kath was asked if she would go down and pray with Freda and then give her a tablet so that she would be able to sleep whilst the rest of the family were at the funeral.

Kath took our girls to stay with one of our neighbours so that she could go and see Freda. I arrived back at Bristol's Temple Meads Station later that Tuesday. Kath met me and filled me in regarding the day's events. I suggested that we call in and see Freda on the way home as I had not been able to see her for a few days. She lived in an apartment flat with her brother and his family. It was on the fourth floor of a high-rise block of flats.

When Kath and I arrived there was quite a crowd of people outside. There had been a nasty accident. A lady had been knocked down by a car and an ambulance had taken her to the Bristol Royal Infirmary Hospital. As we made our way to the fourth floor I said to Kath, "Wouldn't it be strange if the lady taken to hospital was Freda?"

Such an idea was crazy – Freda was dying of cancer. The brother met us. The lady in the ambulance *was* Freda! She had attended her mum's funeral and then gone to do some shopping!

How on earth could that be possible? It was a complete mystery that would do justice to an Agatha Christie story. There must be a twist in it somewhere.

There certainly was! For all those months, Freda had pretended to be the sister-in-law on the telephone. Indeed, Freda had no sister-in-law in reality. She phoned us every morning to find out the approximate time of our visit so that she could be in bed with her tubes when any of us arrived.

We had all been conned for almost a year. I know it is hard to believe, but I can assure you that this story is true.

There is a very sad side to the story. Freda wanted nothing from us apart from just a little attention. I know that there are lots of people in our world who just crave for a bit of attention and caring love. To add to the sadness of the story, it seems that Freda suffered from a complaint that I understand is called psychogenic. I am told that it causes people to show all the symptoms of their imaginary illness.

I remember so very well when Kath and I were on another visit to South Africa. The programme they had planned for us had been a fairly hectic one. We both felt it would be good if we could have our route home changed so that we could spend a few days in Lisbon, Portugal. The airline kindly arranged this for us. We arrived in Lisbon around midday.

Boasting springtime temperatures during the winter and cool summers freshened by a breeze blowing in from the Atlantic, the capital of Portugal since its conquest from the Moors in 1147, is a legendary city. When we arrived, radiant skies brightened the monumental city, with its typical tile-covered building façades and narrow medieval streets.

It was super weather. We found a nice hotel and booked in for two nights. There was time for a walk before the evening meal, so we went down to the harbour. A smart looking man was selling some watches. He actually had some Omega watches for sale. I have a weakness that can truly be called 'looking for bargains'. Here was a chance to find one. He was selling the top of the range Omega watches for just $100, which at that time was only about £50. I had the feeling that Kath was glad I didn't have $100 to spend. We moved away from the area of temptation and made our way to a café to enjoy a cup of coffee. We had only just sat down when our watch salesman came in.

He said, "As you are from Britain, sir, I will let you have it for $50."

That certainly was a bargain price for an Omega watch but I didn't have $50. We went to a nearby park and sat down. It was not long before our salesman friend arrived. He tried to convince me that he really wanted me to have the watch. For my part I tried to convince him that I only had $19 left. To my amazement, he murmured something that seemed to indicate that the deal was on. He went away with my $19 and I went away with my Omega watch. When we arrived home in England, I was delighted to show the family and friends the result of the bargain deal I had struck in Lisbon.

A few weeks later I called in at the local jewellers and asked for his opinion. I called back the next day.

"Mr Jones," he said, "that is a genuine Omega face, but I have never seen such rubbish behind a watch face in all my life."

Another so-called bargain had been a hoax. I gave it to a friend of mine for his young son to play with. The following Sunday, I preached on "All that glitters is not gold and all that appears Omega is not Omega". It all reminded me of the clever and cunning devices of the devil and how he shows us the face of fun, enjoyment, pleasure and make-believe life, but he does not show us that behind the sham face that he presents there is the sting of death. The Bible makes very clear to us the real truth. Christ said, *"It's the broad way that ends in destruction!"*

I am so glad that one day many, many decades ago, I found the 'narrow way' that leads to TRUE LIFE.

CHAPTER 18

It's a Small, Small World.

It was early in 1970 that I was invited to visit our British missionaries in Guyana as part of my presidential tour of some of our overseas Elim churches. John and Gladys MacInnes were outstanding missionaries. They had responded to the call of God when Elim had little or no witness in Guyana.

When my eldest daughter Glenys and I arrived, a number of churches had already been established. The main church was in Albert Street in the capital city of Georgetown. John and Gladys lived in an apartment above the church. John was a man of great vision and unstinting hard work. It is always good to see these two factors working together, and I'm convinced that they were the reason for the success of the work in Guyana. John was an ardent Scotsman whilst Gladys was an equally ardent Welsh lady from Neath (just about nine miles from my home town of Swansea).

One of the first things to strike me was that most of the houses were built on stilts. When I enquired about the reason for this I was told, "The land is below sea level and so our present building plans are an absolute necessity."

This gave a wonderful opportunity for a church to be opened below the house. As Glen and I travelled around the country, we saw that in every case this was exactly what had happened. Latterly, through better drainage in places, some properties are going up from ground level.

Glen and I were there for four wonderful weeks. The weather was hot and humid and when it rained, it *really* rained. I recall the day that Glen and I were in town when one of Guyana's infamous storms broke loose on us. Everyone dashed for cover. That is, everyone except Glen and me. We just stood out in the rain because we simply wanted to get wet through, in order to cool down a bit. I have often wondered what the locals thought about us. Probably, "That foolish couple must come from Britain!" Who could blame them?

Every Thursday at lunchtime we enjoyed a very special meal that immediately took us back to Wales. Gladys cooked super fish-and-chips. We all sat on the balcony of their home and thoroughly enjoyed our fish-and-chips, with salt and vinegar, out of newspaper!

I have already mentioned Sister Tempow and her letter of great encouragement to me when the doctors had just told me that I would never preach again. She had a truly exciting church in Middle Road, La Penitence (not many miles from Georgetown) with an excellent group of young Christian men who later went to various parts of the country and pioneered their own churches.

Pastor Ramdeen was the minister at Agricola. I recall my very first meeting there as I watched the small lizards making their way across the ceiling. I was bodily frightened that one of them would land on my head! Thankfully it never happened. Brother Ramdeen was quite a charismatic character and his church reflected the qualities of its leader.

John and Gladys must have been thrilled when their son Ian and his wife, Valerie, responded to the call of God and joined them in Guyana.

For a very particular reason, I want you now to join me on our visit to the church at Ithica which is on the Berbice river. When Glen and I arrived, the small church was packed to capacity. There was a small table near the back wall of the hall. I had to somehow stand between that table and the back wall. It was a jam. For the very first time in my life, I preached standing almost rigid against a wall. Glen sang a couple of songs and I'm sure the people were blessed, just as they had been at every other church where Glen had sung. I began to preach. It was rather difficult because of my position, but things were going quite well.

Then it started: a tap-tap here and a tap-tap there. The people were tapping their arms, their legs, their necks and their faces. What on earth was happening? I soon found out. It was not long before I was also doing my goodly measure of tapping. A plague of mosquitos gate-crashed our meeting and reached me! I only managed to get halfway through my sermon at that meeting, although it did seem to me that the people were fairly used to that kind of invasion.

Those pesky insects arrived again when I was back in Ithica twelve months later. On that occasion, however, they arrived before I had even started to preach. My soloist, Len Magee, was only on his first solo! This time I made sure that I was fully prepared for such an invasion. I had my socks outside my trousers, a thick scarf around my neck and a body that reeked with TCP medication. It worked for me but not for Len. That night he learned in a painful way the

197

importance of being prepared. Come to think of it, I have never preached a complete sermon at Ithica and right now I'm not particularly keen to try!

Now you must come with me to the colourful and busy Georgetown Market. It was held in a massive place with many, many stalls. The crowd of shoppers was so large that I found it difficult to get near any of the stalls. There was one exception. A short elderly lady was standing by her small stall with not even one prospective buyer taking any interest. I stood by her stall just hoping that with someone standing and looking, others would be prompted to come. She only had cottons, needles and buttons on her stall, but I started to chat with her.

"How's business today, mam?" It was a foolish question really, because I could see it was not very good.

Her cheerful reply was wonderful and I, as a minister of the Gospel of Jesus, learned a tremendous truth from the lips of that little lady that day in Georgetown Market:

"Not too bad sir! You see, *EVERY DAY IS FISHING DAY BUT EVERY DAY IS NOT CATCHING DAY!*"

What a vital truth for every Christian, whether preacher or not. Every day is 'sowing day' but every day is not 'reaping day'. That wonderful principle is both true and greatly challenging. She must have worked to that principle, because she was still in business even though on that particular day there was not a buyer in sight!

One memorable day, John MacInnes took Glen and me to the Leper Hospital in Mahaica on the east coast, about 70 miles from Georgetown. At that time, part of the journey was on primitive dirt roads. I had never been anywhere like it before and I had never seen anything like it before. I met some remarkable people there who not only made me feel ashamed of myself, but also taught me some important lessons.

For instance, there was Alice. A small, rather shrivelled-up little lady who was suffering so badly with leprosy that I was convinced that she didn't have much time left on Earth.

She spoke in feeble tones: "Brother Jones, when you go back to England, make sure you tell them that Jesus is coming again!" I still try to make sure that I do.

John took me into a long ward with a concrete floor and uncomfortable-looking beds. As far as I could see, there was no one in that ward. We went down to the very last bed on the right-hand side. There was Hannah sitting on her stumps by the side of the bed. When I looked more closely I saw that Hannah had no fingers. There were just stumps. In her mouth was a needle; in the part of her hands that remained she was holding a piece of some kind of cloth. Her head moved from side to side. Hannah was making a rug.

John MacInnes had an ingenious plan. People from the British homeland would send him copies of their weekly magazine entitled "The Elim Evangel". He had built an area in his office where they could be stored. They went back over the period of the previous twelve months. So it was that when we visited Hannah, John had a copy of the Evangel in his hand. It was dated exactly the same week twelve months previously. Hannah had put down her rug and took the needle from her mouth.

John asked me to pray and then, turning to Hannah he said, "Hannah I have brought you the Evangel." Many times since, in memory, I have seen those leprous hands reaching up to grasp the Evangel (the good news of the Gospel message) and an outstanding missionary reaching down his hand to put it into those leprous stumps. That evening, it hit me: sin is a soul-destroying leprosy. God has entrusted to His Church the good news of the Gospel of Christ (the Evangel). We must pass it on or else we fail God and our generation. THAT MUST NEVER HAPPEN!

It was at the same hospital that I met Cameron, one of the most amazing men I have ever had the privilege to meet. There was a really beautiful chapel in the grounds of the leper hospital, which seated about 100 people.

That particular afternoon the chapel was full. The singing was good. Len Magee sang a couple of songs and the people loved it. It was then that John said, "Now Cameron is going to tell us what good things the Lord Jesus has done for him."

I looked at Cameron more closely. He had no fingers, only stumps. His face was badly marked; his lips swollen and his mouth terribly twisted. Cameron was certainly not a pretty sight. My eyes looked up to meet his eyes, but they never did. Cameron didn't have any eyes. There were only empty sockets! What was there for him to be thankful for to anybody?

He had been baptised in the nearby river on the previous Sunday. Cameron stood to his feet. I could hardly believe what I was hearing. "I have no hands to hold with and no eyes to see with. But I thank God that I am anchored to the Rock of Ages."

That testimony was terrific and so very moving. Amazingly, that was not the end. John said, "Now Cameron will sing for us."

What did this man have to sing about? How would he manage to sing with such a twisted mouth? Cameron stood to his feet again. There was no music. He just pitched the note himself and sang a song that I immediately recognised as the Bill and Gloria Gaither classic, "He Touched Me". I had heard it before, of course, sung by top-rated gospel artists. I had also heard first-class American choirs sing it. But I never heard anyone sing it as Cameron did that day. He began:

"He touched me, Oh He touched me
and oh the joy that floods my soul,
Something happened and now I know,
He touched me and made me whole."

My heart pounded, my eyes moistened, I was humbled as tears ran freely down my face. I realised, as never before, how very blessed I was and that I was not nearly as grateful as I should be. I determined that day that I would seek to be more grateful to the One who has so graciously and freely poured out His manifold blessings on me. Those blessings are new every morning!

Six thousand miles away from the City Temple in Bristol is the Full Gospel Church in Durban, South Africa. I was there for three months. A goodly-sized welcome party of ministers met me in the airport. They decided that I needed a meal.

One brother said, "We know exactly where the airport restaurant is and that has just what you like!"

Finally seated in the establishment, I looked at the menu. I was both amazed and delighted at the same time. There was no 'or' anywhere on it. One could have every item on the long menu if one's appetite and stomach could cope with it. I was sorry that, at that moment, neither my appetite nor my stomach could cope. It seemed to be the same pattern and practice in every other SA restaurant and there were a number of times when I made my mouth equal to the opportunity!

South Africa is noted for its gold mines. Predictably, I was taken down one of these. We descended in a cage, and having arrived at the mine itself I felt that the word 'cage' was very apt.

The wages of the mine-workers were very small, but most of them were not South Africans but rather workers from other nearby African countries. They would come to work there because the wages were a great deal more than in their own country. They would usually stay in South Africa for about eighteen months and then return to their families and homes feeling mighty rich.

I sometimes recall my first meeting in the country. The church was in the smallish town of Springs. That evening there was a thunderstorm, the like of which I had never seen or heard before or since in all my life. It was accompanied by hailstones that the local paper said were the size of golf balls. Truly, they were pretty big. Certainly, I have never seen hailstones that size before. We left the home where I was staying about half an hour before the church meeting was due to start. I found it rather a frightening journey. Why hadn't they cancelled the meeting? There wouldn't be many there anyway, I thought ... The church was packed.

The itinerary they had planned for me took me to most parts of the country. Durban has a superb beach and enjoys 320 days of sunshine each year, but the weather can be very humid, almost unbearable. The pastor, Reverend Jack Wooderson and his wife had moved to South Africa some years previously and were the ministers of this very flourishing Full Gospel Church. The church in Durban was the first church I saw with a mixed congregation and even then those who were not white had to sit in the balcony.

As many people say, it really is a small, small world. At the end of one of the meetings in Durban, a lady came up to me and her very first words were, "Some of us feel that we have known you all our life. We had heard so much about you."

She went on to explain. "We have some lovely friends who moved to South Africa from England some years back. They committed their lives to Christ in your church in Bristol. It was through their friendship and witness that my husband and I came to faith in Christ."

Over the years my visits to South Africa were many and on most of the occasions I was glad that Kath was able to be with me. We were conscious of the Lord's blessing and presence. It was in South Africa that Kath and I saw a most wonderful miracle of healing in answer to prayer. I must make it clear that I am writing about DIVINE HEALING ... GOD HEALING.

A lady came into one of the meetings and told us her story. After a thorough medical examination, it was confirmed that the baby this young mother-to-be was carrying had died within her. Arrangements had already been made for her to go into hospital to have the dead foetus removed. She came forward for prayer. The congregation and I united in prayer that God would bring her baby back to life. During that same night the lady was wakened by the resurgence of the young life within. The following morning she went back to the hospital for a further examination.

This miracle of Divine healing was later confirmed by the very specialist who had advised her to have the baby removed as soon as possible! At the right time, a healthy baby was born.

There is one simple little incident that I remember well, probably because I have used it as a sermon illustration more than once. I had not arrived in South Africa. I had not even boarded the plane at London's Heathrow airport. I was waiting in the queue at Heathrow for the coaches that would take us out to the plane. The coaches were all filled almost to overflowing. There was just me and a young lady about 16 years of age left. I asked her where she was going. She told me, and I thought it was certainly a long way for a youngster to travel on her own.

I ventured a question: "Are you nervous about flying?"

I knew for sure that there were moments when I was a little nervous about it.

"No!" she replied.

I said, "Not even a little bit?"

It was with firm conviction that she said, "No, I'm not the least bit afraid, MY DAD IS THE PILOT."

That ended our conversation. But I was reminded, yet again, of the tremendous truth that MY HEAVENLY DAD IS

THE PILOT TOO! The words of the old Negro spiritual flooded into my mind:

> *"He's got the whole wide world in His hand,*
> *He's got you and me brother in His hand,*
> *He's got the whole world in His hand."*

I am so glad that He has.

Kath and I were greatly blessed in our own lives during our preaching visits to Norway, Holland, USA, Canada, Mexico, Sweden and Finland. Truly, it is a small, small world and it seems to get smaller each year.

It was during the time that I was General Superintendent that my friend Wynne Lewis and I felt that we should accept an invitation to visit Poland for a series of meetings. Quite remarkably, the communist government's Minister of Religion had granted us a permit to travel to many parts of the country. We simply had to seize this golden opportunity to preach the gospel behind the Iron Curtain.

From the shores of England, we made the thirty-six hour journey to Warsaw by boat and train. The train journey was horrendous. We stopped at every possible checkpoint and frontier. There was no buffet car on the train, neither was there any heating. Were there any loos, we wondered, beginning to feel a bit desperate. What a relief! Yes, there were a couple of them on the train!

The Cold War still maintained its chilling threat to the fragile peace. It was a most unusual invitation to the dour capital of this once proud eastern European state, held since

1945 in the tight grip of Soviet communist domination. British evangelists were very rarely given even a passing whiff of an invitation into this bastion of socialist experimentation deeply behind the fearful Iron Curtain.

It was bitterly cold when we arrived in Warsaw amid deep snow. We were met by our kind host at the uninspiring rail station, and although he was certainly well prepared for the conditions, with his extra warm hat and clothing, Wynne and I were certainly not!

We were driven through miles and miles of poor, bleak, grey streets as he took us to his modest home. We were both tired and cold. He showed us our bedroom. It was massive.

He pointed out to us the two beds that we should use. They were at the far end of the bedroom. We soon hit our pillows and I'm sure we were both still fast asleep when there was the sound of our bedroom door opening. It was a man and a woman and eventually they got into the bed at the other end of the bedroom. We discovered next morning that the couple were friends of our host and that they were on their honeymoon.

We visited and preached the Gospel in many of the towns including Wraclaw, Olencia and Warsaw. Each evening by six o'clock, every hall where we were preaching was already packed to capacity. The people's hunger for the Word of God was very real, almost tangible. It was amazing that the dear folk were never in a hurry to disperse. They were quite happy for the meetings to go on for two or three hours.

Large groups of young people in their teens and twenties were also asking for extra meetings so that they could chat with us about the vibrant life that Christ Jesus could give.

Both Wynne and I were thrilled at what we saw and what we experienced. Preaching about the Love of Jesus to many folk who were hearing the real Gospel for the first time, was as thrilling as it could get.

One of my special friends in Norway is Hans Myrvold. I recall the day when Hans spoke to me, as we casually bumped into each other outside the large conference hall in Holland where I was to be the guest preacher that same evening. He said, "Brother, have you ever thought about Russia?"

Raising my eyebrows, I smiled as I replied, "Not really."

He then told me of his hair-raising exploits and the number of underground churches that he was seeking to help. He was keen to get study Bibles into the Soviet Union in order to help the young and inexperienced believers. I think he saw me as a door to get churches in Britain involved in his vision.

It worked, and very soon certain churches in Britain were linked with churches in Russia. In those months that followed, we managed to get hundreds of Bibles into Russia. Hans has his own printing business and managed to take in very basic printing facilities a bit at a time. This was the period when it was neither safe nor popular to have Russia on your list of countries to do evangelism and talk about Jesus Christ. Eventually, the Russian press wrote ominously about my Norwegian friend, describing him as a dangerous man. They nicknamed him "Uncle Hans", and he was never granted another visa to enter the Soviet Union.

In Norway, on more than one occasion Hans and I

travelled the length and breadth of the country. Our less-than-reliable transportation was sometimes in large planes and sometimes in ten-seater ones where luggage was held on one's lap. There was a little doubt that entered one's mind on many occasions: would the plane make it over the top of the next small mountain?

Other times, transportation would be by car or by train. The towns where we had the privilege of preaching the Gospel were too many to list. Amongst them, however, was memorable Hammerfest, that I understand is the northernmost town in the world. The city lies 70° 39' 48" north and achieved its town status on 7th July 1789, making it the oldest town in northern Norway.

Despite its geographical position, Hammerfest has maintained its international connections. As early as 1852 the first international measurement of the earth's circumference was completed in Hammerfest, and in 1891 Hammerfest was the first town in northern Europe with electric street lighting. I sensed a unique atmosphere in this modern city where the town square and harbour are its natural meeting places, ideal starting points for coastal and other scenic excursions amid outstanding natural scenery including waters teeming with fish.

The members of the churches who had united for the three-day series of meetings had prepared well, both by prayer and advertising. There were excellent congregations. No hype of any kind to try and "work up" the atmosphere of any meeting.

I cannot say that there were many first-time commitments to faith in Christ, but it was good to see God moving in the lives of many Christians as they came forward, some with tears, to make a new commitment to Christ. Our accommodation was in a super self-catering apartment. Hans did the shopping, and Kath did the cooking. I have to confess I did little or nothing in either department.

From Hammerfest we moved on to Alta, where it was very very cold. On our first visit it was quite a small town with a large fishing industry. The members of the church where we were to hold the series of meetings were quite thrilled to have a visit from a British preacher. They had prayerfully prepared for the meetings. The church was quite an attractive building and it was packed for the three evening services.

As in Hammerfest there was a great move of God amongst the Christians. There were tears and there were renewed commitments. Their biggest problem at Alta was that they found it almost impossible to keep any pastor for a long period, because it was one of the towns where one lived in six months of light followed by six months of darkness. The most amazing fact to me was that the townsfolk could tell me the exact date and day when the period of light would begin and the exact day it would end; and when I say "the exact day" I really mean the exact day. It was almost uncanny! They were very keen for us to return the following year – which we did. However, we did make very sure that our visit was during the six months of light!

The Philadelphia Church in the capital city of Oslo was completely different. It is a large modern church building seating up to 1,500 people. There was enthusiasm, exhilarating congregational singing and an abundance of musical talent, including a large choir and a brass band of around fifty members.

It was the members of the band who later invited Kath and me to accompany them on their visit to Russia. I was to be padre to the band and the preacher at all the meetings. Kath and I were always blessed in our own Christian life in Philadelphia. The only pointer I have regarding our being a blessing to them is that in our eleven visits to Norway they always wanted to be included in our itinerary for each visit. Kath and I rejoiced to see a goodly number of people coming to faith in Christ during our visits there.

I still remember one of my most embarrassing moments in Norway. It was the Friday night of the annual conference of the Pentecostal churches. To my surprise they asked me to speak at their missionary rally that evening. It was only a few months after our missionaries and their children had been massacred in Rhodesia. I related the story of how 21 terrorist guerrillas came into the missionary compound and brutally murdered everyone.

I could not understand why some of the younger ministers were tittering and were obviously having difficulty in not turning it into a real laugh. I speedily assessed them as not even being fit to be ministers. No compassion, no sensitivity. I found it difficult to continue and almost arrived at the point where I wanted to rebuke them publicly.

All was explained at the close of the missionary rally, Some of them came to me to apologise: "We are really sorry about what happened when you were preaching, but every time you said GUERRILLA your interpreter said GORILLA!"

After telling them what I had thought, I forgave them on the spot.

We had some excellent meetings on our many visits to Norway. I have to confess that I would have loved to see more people coming to faith in Christ. However, I did see how very easy it is for Christians to fall into a spirit of complacency and therefore need, from time to time, a new touch from God, and we did see the Spirit of God at work in hundreds of lives. I remembered that I had made a promise to God many years earlier that every time I preached I would seek to encourage, inspire and challenge every listener. I have sought to keep that promise ever since.

CHAPTER 19

To Russia and China with Love

I have already mentioned the large Philadelphia Pentecostal Church in Oslo. And having heard their brass band play at the services I speedily understood why they had won a number of brass band contests.

It was one day in 1983 when I received a phone call from Oslo. It was Tom, the man who arranged all the tours for the band. "Pastor Jones, we are planning to go to Russia later this year and we would like you to come with us as padre to the band and as the preacher. We have already made arrangements for a good interpreter. Will you pray about the prospect please?"

About six months later Kath and I met up with about fifty band members and friends. It was then to Finland by air. Then over to what was then named Stalingrad in the Soviet Union. To my surprise, it was a smallish airport and it took us over three hours to get through customs. I have to admit that the extra time became necessary from the customs point of view because we did have in the band-cases, besides the instruments, 8,000 Gospels of John and 120 Bibles in the Russian language. On the same visit we took a couple of hundred bars of soap. At that time, we understood that the Russian common folk were receiving just one bar of soap every three months. We also remembered to take stocking tights for distribution to the Russian ladies and chewing gum for the children.

Two coaches were awaiting us and our first destination was Tallin. Our first Christian service was in a large old-fashioned, dirty-grey Cathedral with a congregation of around 500. Then our next meeting was into a clearing in the woods and a tin shack where about 50 people were awaiting us. They were simply great, fired-up, singing with great enthusiasm and eager for the Word of God, so that we had great difficulty in getting away.

The evening was spent in the large public square in Tallin. We were told that it was the first open-air meeting to be held in that square for many years, so there was evidence that the cold Iron Curtain control was melting. I was sure that it was the presence of the brass band that made it possible. I simply did a little speaking between the items. One man spoke to me through my interpreter. He then went home to fetch an old hymnbook that he wanted me to have. The reason, he said, was because I had told them about Jesus. Emotionally, I still cherish that well-worn hymnbook today.

We held meetings in many other Soviet towns, including a large tent meeting in Riga. By midweek, nearly all the Gospels of John had gone and so had the Bibles. Russian people were queuing for them and reaching out their hands to receive them just as if they were food parcels. In reality, that's truly what they were! The dear folk were so grateful and were always keen to present Kath with flowers. I treasure the superb photo of her included in this book on the next page, that was taken by someone at the close of a meeting during our visit to Russia.

Kath in the Soviet Union

receive Jesus into their life to come forward and kneel around the large platform. I fully realised that I was taking a risk and faced the possibility that no one would come forward. Instantly, large numbers of folk came right out and knelt down. Members of the band reckoned that there were about one hundred and fifty at the front. To my shame, I was so surprised that I thought they had completely misunderstood me, and proceeded to repeat some of the message and invited those who had misunderstood to return to their seat.

Not one person moved. It so happened that one member of our party had just two hundred Gospels of John left and so at least one hundred and fifty people went away with a copy. It was so thrilling and exciting. Yet at the same time it was very humbling to see God move in such a remarkable way in Russia.

On the Monday morning, we arrived back in Oslo in time for lunch. It was then home to Bristol for Kath and me. Those times in Russia will always live in my memory.

There is one quite sad event that I need to recount. My friend Hans, who had done lots of the planning and made most of the contacts, went and collected all our visas without a single problem. But there was no visa for Hans. He was still on the Soviets' blacklist! I have no doubt, however, that God made sure that Hans received a double blessing. I truly believe that our gracious God does things like that!

When I resigned as General Superintendent, mainly on health grounds, my conference colleagues were kind enough to give Kath and me air tickets so that we could have a good, restful holiday. The package also included hotel accommodation which was excellent.

It was very cold when we left Heathrow Airport at 5.45 pm. Our first stop was in the warmth of Singapore, which is both an island and a country, but perhaps its best description is that of city-state. Its combination of Western-style development and Eastern-style calm seems to present the best of both hemispheres. It's a modern metropolis. There we met some super Christians. They laughed as we attempted to eat the excellent Chinese food with chopsticks. I was a complete failure!

The Asian churches at which I had the privilege to speak were small but spiritually vibrant. One could sense a great hunger for the Word of God. We were there in Singapore for just four days and then moved on to Thailand. That country had so much to catch our interest. The chaotic but fascinating capital of Bangkok was alive with commerce and street-bustle nearly every hour of the day. Whether either the city or the country were generally safe, I am not sure. Nevertheless, Thailand is among the most visited countries of the world.

Gazing over the skyline, poverty and wealth were apparent from the same bedroom window in the hotel. One of the most interesting events was our visit to the Floating Market. We witnessed appalling poverty. It comprised rough wooden shacks all along the banks of the river. They were built on stilts simply because it was more profitable for the 'shopkeepers' to use whatever land was available for growing produce. This was more important to them than building a house. Most of the families owned just a small boat. The people did the washing of their clothes and also bathed themselves in the rather dirty river.

At one point we passed a Buddhist temple. One of the buildings was used for cremation and immediately next door there was a coffin factory. Being in Thailand gave us the opportunity of inviting two of our young missionaries to our hotel. They were quite thrilled at seeing us and we trusted that our time with them brought some blessing and encouragement to them. Our stay in Thailand was again four days and then it was "Hong Kong, here we come!"

Hong Kong came under British administration as a direct result of the Opium Wars of the 19th century. When peace terms were drawn up in 1841 at the Treaty of Nanking, the Emperor of China agreed that Britain should have an insular trading base, but the name of the island was left blank until ratification in the following year, by which time Hong Kong was already a thriving British-run harbour. The territory was handed back to the Chinese in July 1997. Hong Kong is now a Special Administrative Region of the People's Republic of China.

A missionary friend, Paul Sachet-Waller and his wife Sue met us at the airport. They had certainly prepared for our visit. Paul seemed to have entirely forgotten that this was supposed to be a restful holiday. He had planned meetings just about every other night. There were some thriving churches and at one meeting there was a congregation of around 1,300. Once again there were plenty of boats of all shapes and sizes and certainly plenty of hot Chinese food.

The next part of our journey was very carefully planned by Paul. We proceeded to the airport and in 25 minutes we were in China, each of us with quite a large suitcase. They were much too big for a two-night stay but just the right size for 150 Bibles in each. Paul and Kath moved quickly through customs with no problem. It was my turn. Very politely the young Chinese inspection lady said, "Will you kindly open up your case sir?"

I immediately knew I was facing a problem. In memory, I can just see her stacking up my 150 Bibles as she spoke. "You are not supposed to do this sir!"

I mumbled something that I had read in a newspaper about increased religious freedom in China. My ploy didn't work. She kindly gave me two back for myself with the firm words: "You can collect the others on the way out, sir."

As we were planning to return to Hong Kong by train, I dared to suggest to the inspector that she could give them to some of her friends. Kath and Paul were anxiously waiting for me to join them. Paul booked a taxi to take us to the hotel.

The cab driver picked up Paul's case. It was a bit of a struggle – which was understandable. It did have 150 Chinese Bibles in it. He had just the same kind of struggle with Kath's case. Then he came to mine. He prepared himself for another heavy heave. He nearly toppled over and nearly dropped my case, it was so light. It had not much more than a pair of pyjamas and a toothbrush in it!

We were soon at the hotel and well settled in our room. Paul said, "A few friends will be coming along tonight."

He had at least twenty friends lined up, and they all seemed to have rather discreet small bags with them! I spoke for a short while on the 'Baptism in the Holy Spirit'. We prayed together and some of those Chinese Christians went away that night with a new experience in God. I should add that they also went away with about twenty Bibles each in their small discreet bags. Kath and I began to wonder about Paul's plans for the next day.

After a good night's sleep we soon found out. His first words next morning were, "I know a nice place where we can have a nice cup of coffee!"

That sounded really good. But we wondered why on earth did he have that blue backpack with him?

There were bikes, bikes, and more bikes everywhere. Paul was right about a "nice place" for coffee. And the coffee? Well, that was fairly good. We hadn't finished drinking it when a smartly-dressed man with a blue backpack came in. I thought to myself, most surely, he must have bought that blue backpack in the same stores as Paul; they were identical. We finished our coffee. It was 'loo time'. They joined each other in the small room for gents complete with their blue backpacks.

In my mind, I said to myself, "Surely, they haven't done a change of backpacks?" ... Most surely they did!

Later, one of Paul's friends told us the amazing and humbling story of one man who had walked for two days simply to be where he could get a Bible. He told of the difficulty of getting any Bibles into the small underground church where he worshipped. They had worked out their own plan for using just one Bible. It was simple. They just tore out the pages and shared them out among themselves. The next time they met they would just exchange pages! Ashamed, I thought of my bookshelves at home. On them was just about every translation there was available. When

221

we heard that story, Kath and I realised that our love and appreciation of the Word of God should be greater than ever before. It reminded us in a new way of the preciousness of God's Word.

Soon it was back to Hong Kong and a final meeting before the plane took us on to Honolulu. This time for rest only. Truth to tell, I was forced to rest with an attack of pneumonia!

By the way, we never did get those Bibles back that we left at the Chinese border control. We returned by train. Quite a few times after, Kath and I wondered if the nice young customs lady-inspector gave any Bibles away to her friends. We will never know the answer to that! ... Or will we?

Russia and China were just about the last long-haul trips that we did together. The travel was simply tremendous and the wonderful memories of it live with me today.

CHAPTER 20

What Now?

We moved from Bristol to Caerphilly for our retirement at a rather difficult time. We had a super bungalow in Bristol and our eldest daughter Glenys, together with her husband Paul and son Chris were moving back from Cheltenham and they had purchased a bungalow immediately around the corner from us. The situation was perfect.

Our concern, however was for the pastor and his wife who were following us to the Bristol church. We did have a fear that our being there after so many years might make it a little more difficult for them.

When we moved back to Caerphilly, we did wonder sometimes whether it was a mistake. God helped us in that question. Only a few months had passed when Pastor John Cooper and his church leadership invited us to become part of the ministry team. It was simply great, and the privilege of working with John Cooper was a bonus. When John had been in college, his great ambition had been to come and be my assistant at the Bristol City Temple. The roles were now reversed. I was his assistant at Caerphilly. Kath and I were so very happy and fulfilled. John Cooper was a great man of God and his wife Carol was an absolute gem. The church was progressing well.

Then tragedy struck. John was stricken down with a brain

tumour. The pain he suffered I shall never forget. Months passed by. His condition grew worse and – after a number of months – God called him home. It was one of the most moving thanksgiving services that I have been in and certainly one of the most difficult to conduct. The tributes to John Cooper were moving, and all the more so, because they were true to his Godly life.

A new minister had to be appointed to the local Caerphilly Elim Church and our ministry at Caerphilly, on a regular basis, came to an end.

By this time Kath's health was deteriorating and she was becoming much frailer. The problem was increased by the difficulties with my own health condition. I had to be in various hospitals for eight weeks as they tried to sort out my pneumonia condition.

I recall one day in particular when I was feeling quite low in spirit. A young man named Jeff Brown came to visit me. We chatted about his work and about the services that he had conducted over the recent weeks. Just before he left I asked him to pray for me. His reply was quite amazing: "Certainly Pastor Jones; but before I pray, I want to give you a message that I feel the Lord gave me for you. It's in Psalm 118:17. *'You shall not die, but live, and declare the works of the Lord'."*

That message was certainly from God and it was most certainly for me. Our daughters and friends were marvellous. They came and stayed with Kath night after night while I was in hospital.

Sometime after our return from our foreign trips, our Kath suffered a serious heart failure. Fortunately, however, we were still able to stay on in our lovely Caerphilly bungalow home where, whatever window we looked through, we could always see to the beautiful surrounding hills. The Caerphilly people were so kind to us that we actually got the feeling that they really wanted to keep us there.

We realised that this situation could not continue. We made contact with a superb residential retirement home (sometimes even called a hotel). It is just one of two such establishments in this country although the American company has hundreds of them in the USA and Canada. Looking out from our new home's window, we could have a superb view of the sea front.

Kath and I had to sell our Caerphilly bungalow. The first people who viewed it, bought it at the asking price. We moved into our new home in the residential retirement home in Clevedon in June 2000. We were living there when Kath passed away and I am still there.

It was a completely new lifestyle for us both in Clevedon and it took us some little time to settle in. We still tried to do everything together and so I only accepted preaching engagements that were near at hand.

One great problem was that the residential home was non-Christian and even non-religious. We prayed fervently that God would use us in our new surroundings for His glory. Nothing happened for months. We then felt that we should make some attempt to do something worthwhile, if only to test the waters.

We planned for a Sunday evening "Songs of Praise". It was a success. The Lord blessed the effort. Then *something quite remarkable happened!* The local management offered

We prayed fervently that God would use us.

me a building that could be turned into a lovely chapel seating up to 35 people.

The chapel is never used for any other activity but we can use it for any service at any time. We now have nine meetings each month including four prayer meetings, four Tuesday morning meetings, one "Songs of Praise" and one "Sunday half hour". There are around 90 residents here and at least 33% attend some of the services each month and appreciate them. I am so glad that God allowed Kath to see something of the answer to our united prayers. I feel like a pastor/evangelist again!

In 2005, I still have the privilege of conducting interviews with Christian people from all walks of life for the Vision Channel on Sky digital TV.

A few months after Kath and I arrived in Clevedon, a local church invited me to be involved as an associate pastor, where we are seeing spiritual and numerical growth. In addition to this I have the added joy of ministering week-ends in various churches. The Lord is so very gracious to me. I sometimes find it difficult to believe it and even more difficult to understand why. There is one thing that I certainly do know, and it is summed up in the words of blind Fanny Crosby's Victorian testimony-hymn:

> All the way my Saviour leads me;
> What have I to ask beside?
> Can I doubt His tender mercy,
> Who through life has been my guide?
> Heavenly peace, divinest comfort,
> Here by faith in Him to dwell!
> For I know whate'er befall me,
> Jesus doeth all things well.

It was Easter time in 1998 that the first real evidence of Kath's illness came to light. On the surface, it seemed the same as any previous Easters. I was preaching at a series of Easter meetings in Mansfield, England. As usual Kath came with me. She loved meeting people and chatting with them at the door as they left. There were seven meetings over that weekend. Kath was at every one. On the Tuesday when we started our journey home, she didn't seem too well.

On the Wednesday, we arrived home. I sent for our doctor, who immediately called an ambulance. Within half an hour, Kath was in hospital. It was heart failure.

She was in and out of hospital over a period of eight weeks and eventually recovered sufficiently to return home, although very weak. Our lifestyle changed. Our travelling days were at an end. My weekend bookings had to be near at hand as for a few years we still did everything together.

It was Monday, June 10th 2002 at around 10.00 am that she collapsed on the bed. I sent for our doctor. He came quickly and made every effort to resuscitate her. By 10.30 am that Monday morning, my dear Kathleen had gone to be with Jesus.

Ten days later the thanksgiving service for her life and witness was held in the Bristol City Temple where we had been the ministers for almost thirty-two years. The church was packed. It was truly a service of thanksgiving and triumph. Many tributes were rightly paid.

One of the most moving tributes was the one paid by our eldest daughter, Glenys. To the crowded congregation, she said, "Being in a room with Mum was like turning on a light. Her love, support and encouragement were the bedrock of our lives. As we grew up, she was always there. She was there in our disappointment to lift us up with her wise counsel. She was there in our joys, rejoicing with us. She prepared us for life and all that it would bring. We knew that she was praying for us every day that we would be led and guided by our Heavenly Father. Most importantly, also she prayed that we would know the Saviour whom she loved so deeply and served so completely."

I knew that every word of every tribute paid to Kath that day was true down to the finest details. Kath has now arrived Home and seen her Saviour face-to-face. I just journey on, thanking God for my treasured memories of an outstanding woman of God, His wonderful grace to me throughout my life and the tremendous privilege He has given me to proclaim His life-changing Gospel of good news.

THE GREATEST THING HE COULD DO WAS DIE FOR ME.
THE LEAST I CAN DO IS LIVE FOR HIM.

EPILOGUE

Let Thy Mantle Fall on me

In 2005, there is no denying the fact that world leaders are in crisis and there seems to be no one who knows exactly what is going to happen.

The USA, the most powerful country in world history, was almost brought to a standstill by the events of '9/11' (September 11th, 2001). Since then, Middle Eastern suicide terrorists have nations understandably gripped with fear. It should make us all realise that – in spite of all the latest clever discoveries and our wonderful ability to put men on the moon – a nation's power can be brought to the point of crisis in the space of 30 minutes.

It is sad to say that, generally speaking, the Church in the West is seemingly making little or no impact. As a matter of fact, there are those who tell us that religion is the cause of all the world's ills.

In memory, I go back to 1979 when I was Elim's General Superintendent. My colleagues and I met especially to pray and discuss the world situation and the role of the Church. We clearly saw that Almighty God had not changed and that He still longs to bless His people and make them strong and able to do great exploits in His name. We confessed to the Lord how very much we longed for Him to bless us and use us to do exploits for Him.

Sadly, our problems came when we also saw that it did

not work out like that as often as we wished. If God longed for it and we longed for it, why not?

I found it difficult to sleep that night, because that question haunted me over and over again ... Why not? ... Why not? ... Why not? ...

Awakened, God spoke to me and answered the question in a manner that both startled me and challenged me. It came in the form of verse 3 in Psalm 110:

"... *Your people shall be willing in the day of Your power.*" God seemed to say to me, "You ask the question 'Why not?' I ask the question, 'Are you and are My people in the place that I want them to be? Are you doing what I want you to do?'"

It frightened me. I had a full diary. I was heavily involved with hardly a moment to spare. I believe that it was the Lord who showed me that it was easy for me to consider all that I do to be evidence of my involvement in the Lord's work. I saw that in spite of all the activity it is possible not to be doing what He wants me to do and not be where He wants me to be.

When we do just what we want to do, it brings satisfaction and glory to us. But when we do what He wants us to do, it brings satisfaction and glory to Him. His 'people willing in the day of His power'. That is the secret. We must recognise that it must be His power.

That night I saw as never before that I certainly needed His power. I would like it to be in the way I choose. But I saw afresh that God manifests His power in the way He chooses!

Moses saw God manifest His power in a broken branch

231

that became God's rod! ... The Children of Israel saw that same power manifest in the parting of the Red Sea and in manna from heaven! ... To Joshua, that same power was revealed in tumbling walls, in response to obedience. ... Elijah saw it in fire from heaven and heard it in a still small voice! (One has to listen very carefully to hear a still small voice.) ... To a widow woman and her two sons, that same power was manifest in as many empty vessels as possible being made available, and a little bottle of oil that became a miracle oil well! ... To Peter and John on the way to church, it was seen in a leaping, enthusiastic former cripple! ... To a young lad, it was seeing his picnic sardine sandwiches feeding 5,000! ... To Philip the Evangelist, it was revealed in a mighty revival in Samaria with conversions and healings; but on another occasion, it was God's power manifest as he explained the Scriptures to one needy, hungry soul.

Each manifestation was different. But in every case it was His power!

It is also amazing to see the people and the things that God uses to manifest His power: the jawbone of a donkey ... a stone in a sling ... a few ravens ... a small bottle of oil ... and even a donkey.

Historically, every manifestation of God's power was different: in need, in circumstance, in timing, in purpose and in the instrument used. In every case, however, it was His power.

Sometimes we like to see God's power in nice little parcels that we can handle. But God's power doesn't come quite like that. As I read Psalm 110, I felt that I wanted to see what the psalmist saw:

232

Verse 1. *"You sit at my right hand."* That is where the Lord Jesus is – in the place of authority. All the blessings that come from God to me come through the nail-pierced hands.

Verse 2 sounds a note of great triumph: *"His enemies will become His footstool."* Every alien power will be smashed and He will reign from shore to shore.

But now comes the crunch. *'His people willing'!* With Christ, any day can be the day of His power but what about the day of 'His people being willing'? That certainly is different!

How many of us say: "I am willing Lord, as long as it doesn't make too many claims, and is not too inconvenient to my other activities. By the way, Lord, not too much cross carrying please!"

I saw it many times – that real willingness makes its demands and calls for dedicated preparation. I recall that from time to time, it would be our responsibility – as the Elim Executive Council – to interview missionary candidates. When they told us the country they felt God had called them to, the question sometimes put to them was this: "How are your efforts to learn the language going along?"

The candidate's answer did give us some small idea of their preparation. To just be willing is not enough!

When World War II broke out, I was pastoring in my first church. I truly felt that I should be involved in the war effort in whatever way was possible. Thus I volunteered for the Auxiliary Fire Service. I went along to my first training session, where a very long ladder was put up against a very

233

large building. We trainees had to climb the ladder. I admit I was not very good or confident at ladder-climbing but I did my best. At the top, we arrived on a huge flat roof.

Laid out on the roof were straw-filled objects that were supposed to be people. We were instructed to presume there was a fire and that 'those people' had to be taken down the ladder to safety. I found it a little difficult to get the dangling 'victim' comfortably on my shoulder. Getting on the ladder was even more difficult and the descent was a rather frightening experience. I managed six rungs. I knew we both wouldn't make it. I felt it was going to be 'the victim' or me. Loosening my grip, I had decided my charge had to go.

Wide-eyed, looking downward to the ground that was so many rungs below, the 'victim' was ripped open and masses of straw were scattered all around. I eventually reached the foot of the ladder, red-faced and embarrassed. To my disgrace, the instructor was not at all kind in his summing up of my effort, neither was some of his language. "Young man, you are not to make the type of fireman that we are looking for!"

Then he added something that was abundantly clear: "I do appreciate the fact that you were willing but you were certainly not prepared!"

He was absolutely right. I was willing but certainly not ready or prepared. We must be prepared for the 'Day of His Power'. God has his own way of preparing us and it's not the same for everyone.

Moses saw an Egyptian beating an Israelite slave and killed him. He was willing but certainly not ready or prepared to do it God's way. It took 40 years of preparation, minding his father-in-law's sheep. At long last, he heard the voice of God from a burning bush:

"Come now Moses, I'm sending you!"

It is vital in these dark days that we hear His voice. God is not nearly as concerned about a form of worship as I am. He just wants me to hear His voice and obey it. In this noisy world, there are so many voices that clamour for my attention. There is a mass of sound all around me in video and tape form and in seminar form. We need to hear His voice individually and as churches.

Who would deny that we are surrounded by a world with dire political, economic, spiritual, ethical and moral problems? Because satan is enjoying himself so much, it sometimes might seem that we are living in 'the devil's heaven'. Only God's power will save us from spiritual mediocrity.

When the Master went up from the Mount of Olives, the disciples were bereft. The task of world evangelism must have loomed as big and immovable as Mount Everest – that is, until the Holy Spirit came in power. On that Day of Pentecost, the apostles then exploded into action!

In Shakespeare's play "Julius Caesar", in the famous appeal that Mark Antony made to the citizens of Rome after the death of Caesar by assassination, he held before them the emperor's mantle. It was bloodstained. He dramatically declared, "You all do know this mantle: I remember /The first time ever Caesar put it on. /'Twas on a summer's evening, in his tent".

The crowd loved it. They caught fire with enthusiasm. It was then Mark Antony cried, "Now let it [the bloodstained mantle] work!"

I am convinced that God always wants to shed upon His church the 'Mantle of His Power'. I need it, you need it, and today's 21st century Church needs it desperately!

Nowadays 'Elim @ Bristol City Church' (the former City Temple) has the right vision. They desire to be "a light in the city and a blessing to the nations". To carry this through, we all need to have on the 'Mantle of His Power'. Only then will we be able to be 'His people – willing in the day of His power'!

LET THY MANTLE FALL ON ME

Elijah was God's prophet;
Elisha stood close by,
And ere the prophet left him,
He heard the prophet cry:
"Let thy mantle fall on me."
"Let Thy mantle fall on me;
A double portion of Thy Spirit, Lord
Let Thy mantle fall on me!"

Then Elijah made the promise
That, if faithful he would be,
His petition would be granted,
And God's glory he would see.

As Elijah rose to Heaven
In a chariot of fire,
He did not forget his servant,
Who expressed one strong desire:

In the Upper Room they waited –
It was the faithful Christian band –
And their prayer was heard and answered
Over in the Glory land.

"Let Thy Spirit fall on me;
Let Thy Spirit fall on me.
The promised blessing may it be outpoured,
Let Thy Spirit fall on me!"

That prayer of early Christians,
Long ago and far away,
Is the cry of all God's children;
And He's just the same today!

(Floyd Hawkins/Copyright Control)